PLEASE JOIN US by the fire in the family room of our Ozark mountain home, to share hot chocolate with melting marshmallows floating on top . . . and to break the bread of friendship together.

It is indeed a privilege to be with you.

ORPHANS AT HOME
© 1988 by Joe White
Published by Questar Publishers, Inc.
Second Printing, 1988

Printed in the United States of America

ISBN 0-945564-01-5

Cover design by Art for Living West

Library of Congress Cataloging-in-Publication Data

White, Joe, 1948-
When so many feel like orphans at home,
it's time to fall in love with your kids again.

**1. Parenting—United States. 2. Parent and child—United
States. I. Title. II. Title: Orphans at home.**
HQ755.8.W475 1988   306.8'74   88-18211
ISBN 0-945564-01-5

When so many
feel like

Orphans
at
Home

...it's time to FALL IN LOVE
with your kids again

Joe White

QUESTAR PUBLISHERS, INC.

PHOENIX

I WANT TO OFFER deep expressions of gratitude to my dear Mom, for always making our house a home; to Thomas Womack, for his editing skills and admirable character; to Gary Smalley and Josh McDowell, for their loving hearts and wisdom in helping me develop this book; and to Johnny Koons, for running the show while I took time off to write.

CONTENTS

To Trevor

Like a giant oak,

your memory will outlive us all

As I COMMENCE writing a book that I frequently have prayed will affect every aspect of parenting for every mother and father who read it, a familiar lump nags within my neck, making difficult a simple swallow.

The lump in my throat is a tumor I've grown to appreciate. Surgically it is impossible to get to anyway . . . for it's a lump of grief, accompanied often by watery eyes and an empty heart. I'm lonesome for a man who was my second daddy, and who was killed in a plane crash only months ago.

To Dr. Trevor E. Mabery, my encourager, my "other" father, my example, and my friend . . . this book is dedicated.

As he successfully loved two boys and a girl of his own into their young adult lives, Trevor's model as a daddy was unsurpassed. His unconditional love was poured out on his most fortunate family.

He also was a model of success in his profession. So skilled was he that even the famous Dr. Mayo let him perform his most difficult operations when

Trevor was still a young surgeon in the formative years of his career. Small children born with severely deformed faces left Dr. Mabery's operating room with beautiful new eyes, mouths, and noses . . . thanks to this man and his skillful team.

Internationally known and in great demand, Trevor never missed a football game when a son was on the field. For years he and his son rolled newspapers together at 5:30 A.M. for the boy's paper route. During hunting season he and his sons were together in the duck blind or deer stand, weekend after weekend.

His smile never dimmed. He lived always for his God and his family, until the fateful moment when the twin-engine plane he was aboard couldn't climb out of a beautiful Rocky Mountain valley, and crashed into Dead Indian Peak some fifteen thousand feet above sea level.

His reputation as a dad lives on . . . still influencing my life . . . and permeating the pages of this book.

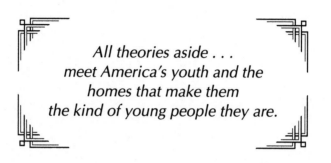

*All theories aside . . .
meet America's youth and the
homes that make them
the kind of young people they are.*

PART I

The Lights Are On, But . . .

*The chains of habit are too weak to be felt
until they're (almost) too strong to be broken.*

—1—

Slipping Away

*We're so busy giving our kids what we didn't have
that we don't take time to give them what we did have.*

*"I hate to sound selfish, like everything's mine.
But please don't get mad when I ask for your time."*

I HIT BOTTOM in my career as a daddy a few summers ago.

I first started realizing it the day my oldest son's babysitter taught him how to ride his bike. It's such a monumental achievement for a boy— in fact, almost four decades haven't erased the memory of reaching that milestone in my own life. But Brady had to experience it without me.

Busy (as usual) with work, I met Brady for a quick lunch that day, and he beamed with excitement as he shared the news.

I had all the right things to say: "Wow, Brady! That's great! I'm so proud of you." Then I added, "Brady, can I come watch you ride your bike later this afternoon?"

The response from this sweet, gentle-spirited six-year-old fell on me like an avalanche. "No, Dad, that's okay. You're busy in the summer."

I'm fighting the tears again as I remember the deep remorse I felt. He had opened my heart more skillfully than a surgeon.

I was losing my son.

He knew it, and I knew it.

In my job as president of a large summer camp complex, I was so busy rescuing other people's kids that my own were drowning. And the problem— as I knew Brady couldn't help but discover as time went on— was that I'm busy not only in the summer but also in the fall, winter, and spring too.

Brady . . . little Brady . . . with the super imagination and the super-sensitivity that's made

It's an alarming moment when it dawns on parents that their child feels orphaned. It's a feeling kids can have at any age, and if you aren't perceptive you may never know it's happening until you find a half-smoked marijuana joint in a jeans pocket on laundry day, or a sexy love note left inadvertently in a desk drawer, or a citation from the local police.

his daddy work harder on smoothing his many rough edges and his hard-driving disposition. With a quick look into the future, I could see Brady as a teenager in someone else's counseling office trying to sort out his bitterness toward a father too busy to show he cared.

NOT LONG AFTERWARD my youngest daughter was attending one of our short-term camps. We agreed to abide by the rule requesting parents not to visit their children for the entire week. (That's tough!)

On the fifth night, Courtney got a touch of homesickness. She began to cry, and her counselor came to her bed to give some hugs and tenderness.

"Corky, don't cry anymore. You'll be home in two days and you'll get to see your daddy and everything."

"I never get to see my daddy!" was her bold protest.

When the week was over, the camp director came to my house. "Sit down," he said abruptly. I sat down, wondering what this was all about.

He told me about the conversation between the counselor and Courtney— little Corky, with long blonde hair and dimples that can't help but melt her daddy's heart. Even when the lower lip is out in an occasional protest, a few tickles and funny faces can bring the dimples back to their rightful place.

"What are you going to do about it?" he asked.

I squirmed. He looked deep into my eyes.

The phone rang. As I went to answer it the intercom buzzed. Then someone came to the door with an emergency. After responding to all three, I sat back down. He was still looking intently at me.

"I asked you, 'What are you going to do about it?' "

"I don't know . . . it's hard . . . there are so many demands . . ."

"Joe, who are the most important people in your life?"

"My family."

"You're not showing it!"

He sat there and didn't give an inch. Finally I agreed to some commitments.

OPEN HEART SURGERY

THIS BOOK is an expression of my gratitude for my months of open heart surgery that summer. To this day I'm carrying out the commitments I made back then. It's still hard. The demands are still there. In fact, they're getting worse. But my priorities are changing. I've aborted almost everything in my life that stands between my children and me. The use-of-time knife has stripped away most of the fat that surrounded the lean meat of necessity.

My wife and I continue the struggle to accomplish more during the necessary hours of daily labor, and in the remaining hours to simply prioritize time with our children over anything else during these years while they're still at home. We're wonderfully amazed that there's adequate time for a few luxuries.

Brady has honestly become my best male friend. I work early and late when he's not available, so that when he comes home I can grab a bat and ball or a go-cart or a fishing rod or a made-up adventure, all for the honor of getting to be by his side for a few golden ticks of the clock. His brother Cooper, and his sisters Jamie and Courtney . . . all of them have become World's Best Companions to me.

ALLOW ME, in love, to ask you the same question the camp director asked me: Who are the most important people in your life?

If it's your family . . . are you showing it?

If not . . . what are you going to do about it?

JUST AS DURING the early days of work on Mount Rushmore, when the explosives engineer was told to blast away all the granite that didn't look like the face of a president, so I urge you to strip away— with dynamite, if necessary— everything in your life that doesn't look like family gold.

☞

—2—

The Champs

Son, you're the greatest!
— Herman "Sleepy" Morgan

*All children are champs—with potential they're packed;
discovery alone is the element lacked.*

ON THAT FATHER'S DAY MORNING, something inside me told me I was being set up.

All four of my children were bubbling with excitement as they led me to their playroom. I felt special to have all that attention from the ones I love the most.

Their eyes sparkled mischievously as they showed me a big white box on the playroom floor, wrapped in fourth-grader uniqueness with hand-drawn decorations on all six sides. It was so BIG!

19

"Hurry, Dad, open it up!"— four little voices screamed in unison, as if from fear the box would pull a self-destruction act before I got to the contents.

As I bent down to pull off the customized wrapping paper, the box began to move, and I heard a whimpering, whining sound from inside. Instantly I knew: I'd been framed!

"There's a puppy inside that thing!" I exclaimed. Soon the lid was attacked by eight tiny hands, and up popped an exuberant ball of black fur.

"Daddy, Daddy, can we keep it?"

"Happy Father's Day, Daddy!"

"Don't you just love him?"

"Let's name him Champ!"

The sounds of excitement filled the house.

I'd been set up to the max. Even their mother was in on the deal. How does a daddy turn down a Father's Day gift— handwrapped in crayon-colored paper, no less?

"Okay, gang," I accepted cautiously, "but only if *you* take care of him."

"Sure, Daddy, we'll be happy to!"

Champ was the sired pup of my big black four-year-old retriever, Pro. Pro, who was from the blood line of Old Yeller, Hollywood's most famous Labrador retriever, now had a major problem: He had to share everything with that

yipping, biting, pestering Champ, who was nothing but an annoyance— to both of us.

Champ may have been my new Lab . . . but
in my heart I didn't really claim him.

OUR NATION'S HOMES are full of little "Champs."
Some are boys, some girls. Some are toddlers and
some are teens. They legally belong to a mom
and/or a dad, but they've never felt totally
claimed.

In various ways they send up their signals
from every city, crying out for unconditional love
and acceptance from their too-busy parents.

Almost every day I get letters from teenagers
across America who feel like little Champ. One
recent letter— from Amy, age seventeen—
epitomizes their cry:

> I've always wanted so badly to please my
> Father and my Mother. I hated to be yelled
> at. Every time I was caught doing some-
> thing wrong, I felt worthless at home and
> at school. It was very embarrassing for me
> to get into trouble. My Mom, who I've
> always been close to, kicked me out of the
> house and started packing my things just
> to get back at my Dad. I kept thinking to
> myself, "Is she serious? Where should I
> go? I have no where to go." The scars run
> pretty deep . . .

DISCOVERY

AFTER PRO AND I had tolerated Champ for a
couple of summer months, an interesting event
forever altered Champ's stature in my heart. The
two dogs were bounding through our summer
camp, with Champ playing his usual game of
jump-up-and-bite-Pro's-neck-lips-and-ears. As
always, Pro used every ounce of self-control in his
pedigree to keep from making supper out of his
menacing offspring.

The two black beauties apparently stopped
alone by our huge outdoor swimming pool— which
was closed for the day— to get a drink, and Pro fell
in. Labradors are born swimmers, but the
distance between the water's surface and the deck
around it was about four inches higher than a dog
can reach. After what must have been fifteen to
thirty minutes, a teenage boy walking by the pool
saw what happened next: As Pro began to go
under, little sixteen-pound Champ leaned down,
bit Pro in the lip, and with some internal shot of
adrenaline pulled his sixty-five-pound daddy out
of the water.

Champ found a new home at our place that
night. Same walls, same roof, same wooden floor,
but it was new. Now he was a hero, and we
treated him as he had deserved to be treated all
along. He was stroked, praised, caressed, and
honored.

Champ now owned a special place in my
heart— a place valued all the more when, two
months later, Pro was struck and killed while
crossing a highway. Now I regard that whim-

pering, oversized box as the best Father's Day present in all the wonderful years since I first received my most cherished title, "Daddy."

Do you have a "Champ" in your home?

After working, counseling, living, and talking with literally hundreds of thousands of teenagers in the past twenty years, I've found that there's a Champ in every one— if that child's parents will only realize it, and discover the vein of gold in their child's heart.

All successful homes have it in common: The Discovery of Champions.

It can be done in all kinds of circumstances, even by single parents. My grandmother found a champion in my mom while raising her all alone. What a job she's done . . . and is still completing, at age ninety-three!

My wife is truly a champion, though her father (a Navy test pilot) was killed when she was four years old. She, too, had a mom who courageously and patiently raised her and her two brothers until a stepdad came into the picture.

My daddy was fortunate to have both parents there at home to do the job, and even more fortunate that both of them recognized his great potential and allowed it to bloom.

The discovery of champions can happen in your family too.

IN THE MONTHS since I began writing this book, our two-year-old Champ has also passed out of our lives. A sudden, tragic death took him seemingly long before his time was due. My only consolation is that before it was too late, we learned to treat him like the champion he was.

Our kids' lives too are so fragile, and the short time we're allowed to be with them races by . . . there never seems to be enough.

Whatever age your children are . . . *today* is a great day to bring out the best in each of their lives.

⚷

Two mothers who wouldn't give up tell the stories of their troubled teenage children ...

Chris's Mom

I SAID it would never happen to my son.

Until his seventh-grade year Chris was polite, loving, and content. When I saw the plastic bag of dried-up leaves in his pocket I didn't even know what it was.

The marijuana habit led to LSD, cocaine, and hash. He lied about it habitually, and I so wanted to believe him— love hopes all things. He made up wild and crazy stories that I wanted to be true. But I couldn't deny the hard facts that followed his footsteps.

His grades went down. He became a skilled player of video games to win drug money, but it wasn't enough. He stole from our home, and burglarized others.

He sold drugs to his friends. While in the ninth grade he was suspended from school for dealing drugs in the library. I was humiliated. I was scared. I wanted him to know I still loved him.

I'm told a common first mistake by parents who learn their child is using drugs is to look the other way and pretend it isn't happening. A second is to look for a quick, easy remedy. A third, when you've tried everything humanly possible and all has failed, is to give up.

We went through stages of all three. But every night we got on our knees in prayer. We'd made mistakes as Chris's parents— no doubt about it. But through it all we loved him while hating his sin.

CHRIS NEVER ran away . . . but I did. The pressure got to me. I checked into a hotel for two nights to struggle with God.

While there I began to see that drugs weren't the enemy. They were just weapons. It was a spiritual battle we were in. The enemy was after my son, my family, my marriage.

I faced all the what if's. I was sure Chris would either commit suicide, die of an overdose, or be killed in a car accident. It was happening in front of my eyes, and I was powerless. I had tried everything, but couldn't rescue him out of his problems.

I decided I would trust God, no matter what. That was the first and best step. I found His peace in that hotel room.

WHEN I WENT HOME things were the same, but I was different.

Chris had become a pro at deceit, a con artist. He hated himself, but on his own he couldn't change. I knew something drastic had to be done. A month at a Christian summer camp helped, but that wasn't enough time. A year at a special home for troubled youth also helped, but even there he smuggled drugs and had the wrong friends.

Then two men who were constructing a Christian camp took Chris in and gave him five months of solitary confinement, hard labor, and love. He would work all day, listen to Christian music and go through Bible studies in the evening, and drop exhausted into bed at 8:00 p.m. The work kept his mind off drugs and built his self esteem, something he drastically needed. Phoning him from home, we continued to pour on the encouragement while making it clear we couldn't allow his former behavior.

Then he came home. He was now

seventeen years old. In another year he would be out on his own. We wanted to believe he was well. But he returned to his old friends, too weak to fight their influence.

Then I heard about Tom Johnson, a wonderful cowboy with a youth ranch in Arkansas. We sent Chris there, and on the way he gave up fighting. Miraculously, all the Christ-centered experience he'd been given, plus our continuing love and unceasing prayers, finally took root in his heart. He asked Jesus Christ to take over his life.

At the ranch he saw an inspirational Christian model in Tom. On the first morning there, at daybreak, Chris helped Tom deliver a newborn calf. As the sun came up, Chris felt as if God was showing him a new life. He didn't tell anyone at the time, because he felt he had talked too much. Now he wanted to show.

He hasn't done a drug since that sunrise.

The next time we saw him, he gave his dad a great big hug.

CHRIS WILL SOON graduate from college.

He shares Christ with druggies and punk rockers. With his skateboard and drums, he gets into places a preacher could never go.

He'll always be on the cutting edge.

Sharon's Mom

WE WERE some of the "beautiful people" in our community— Robert worked night and day while I played tennis at the country club— and our teenage daughter Sharon was an ornament. I had to take time away from my tennis to drive her to school. (Kids deserve better.)

I subtly gave Sharon pressure to stay on top. She just did what I asked her to. When I woke up she was a sizzling sixteen-year-old brunette with big blue eyes and a body filled with alcohol and drugs.

In three hundred and sixty-five days she spiraled down from a "most likely to succeed" to a drunk and a druggie.

No one felt worse about it than she did. She couldn't stop because now her group of friends expected her to live up to her new image. Kids are so totally driven by acceptance. She didn't feel it at home so she got it from whomever she could.

We were so far off as parents. We let the TV set— instead of our example— be our child's value education. If you don't want your kids to drink, don't drink. What you say doesn't matter. Kids learn (or miss learning) responsibility at home.

Things had gotten out of control in such a short time. Robert got scared that we were losing each other over Sharon. "You're giving her too much of your mind," he pleaded with me. "I'm giving her up. We won't fight over her. She's yours now— yours to love, yours to discipline."

I prayed desperately. *Please take her back, Robert.*

Sharon ran.

I felt like someone had shot me with a shotgun and I was full of holes. *I'm bleeding!*

WE GOT her back. Then I tried everything. I played rough at first. I took away all privileges— the phone, the TV set, everything. But the love wasn't there to back up the ultra-strict discipline.

Next I tried to identify with her. I took

her places. I drank with her. I wanted her to see how to drink "responsibly." I was desperate and ready to do anything.

Your heart gets broken during those times. They lie and mislead you. They say it is better and you get kicked. You feel so foolish. She said she hated us, but she was really saying "Help!" She felt so abused and so guilty.

Today she says, "Thanks for not giving up on me after I gave up on myself."

HERE'S HOW the turnaround happened.

Robert and I submitted our whole family to some solid biblical counselors. They told us to keep on believing in Sharon. At first we reacted to that: *"Believe in what?"* But eventually we completely adopted our child in our hearts . . . with all of her problems.

Next, we inventoried our own lives and began to fill our home with consistency. We gave ourselves more lovingly to each other and to our younger children.

I love wine, but when I caught my second daughter and her friends downing some whiskey (from our overstocked liquor cabinet) on their way out of the house to a party, I knew our social drinking had to go too. (Why do we play our kids for such fools sometimes?)

We continued over the next six years to rebuild our ties with Sharon. As we forged the new relationship, we wondered: *How do you go back and undo all the crossed-up circuits?* She had been programmed all wrong.

We didn't quit. We lived on our knees, it seemed.

Sharon protested. "You've never been a mother to me and I can't accept it now." But she did need an authority. I kept my mouth shut and listened to her. Then I would listen some more. When she finished expressing her thoughts, I'd ask, "What are you thinking? . . . What are you feeling? . . . How can I help you?" I filled her with honest praise. Then I'd state my position. Sometimes she'd get so angry.

Robert and I worked at being more honest in everything. We became more available to our kids. In everything we strove to be authentic.

With the help of the Christian youth and family counselors, we began to see daylight. In a couple of years the storm was over and it became only partly cloudy.

TODAY WE ARE CLOSE. Our house is a home. It still rains here sometimes, but there also are sunny days to enjoy.

I believe the tragic years with Sharon actually saved us from a lifetime of casual misery. It was worth the trouble to begin to understand each other and really get to know the power of Jesus Christ in a family.

Today as he left for college, my nineteen-year-old son said, "Mom, wouldn't you rather be called a great mom than a great tennis player or a corporate officer?" Then he added, "You're a great mom!"

Maybe he's exaggerating with the "great." I think "great-ful" (*grateful!*) is a better word for me.

—3—

Who Cares?

Think I'll buy a forty-four / Give 'em all a surprise
Think I'm gonna kill myself / Cause a little suicide.
— Elton John

ELVIS PRESLEY'S colorful step-brother spent some time with us at our sports camp last summer. Elvis loved music, but Rick Stanley loves kids.

As we talked about the plight of the modern teenager, Rick told me of another brother's backstage encounter with David Lee Roth, rock star and teen hero of the late seventies and early eighties who sang of suicide, drugs, torture sex, rebellion, and perversion. After a lengthy conversation about Elvis, his fame, his music, and his tragic death, the brother asked Roth the same question I would want to ask him: "David, what do you think about the thousands of kids out there in the crowd tonight who are getting stoned, wasted, messed up?"

With a blunt, cold stare, Roth answered, "Who cares?"

He's honest. Roth doesn't seem to care about anyone but himself. But the problem is that so many vulnerable kids look up to him. At a typical concert, twenty thousand of them— averaging fourteen years of age— will spend a half million dollars and practically break down the doors to get into two hours of visual and verbal pornography. The next day at school they'll wear their new rock T-shirts to celebrate their evening with a hero.

Who are your kid's heroes?

They're displayed on the posters on the walls of his room. Look into their eyes. What do you see?

A recent survey by America's most popular teen magazine revealed that only 4.1 percent of the teenage girls in America feel they could go to their father to talk about a serious problem. Even more recently, USA TODAY published the eye-opening results of a study of teens under stress. When asked where they turn to for help in a crisis, the most popular choice was music, the second choice was peers, and the third was television. Amazing as it may sound, moms were down the list at number thirty-one, and dads were forty-eighth.

MY BREAKFAST GUEST yesterday was a seventeen-year-old boy who's six-foot-two and weighs a hundred and ninety pounds. He's as lost as a baby billy goat. He comes from a wonderful home, but nine months of the wrong three friends— and who knows how many dozen marijuana cigarettes— have sent him into a tailspin and turned his home upside down. To my amazement, this confused teenager told me over breakfast how both he and his best friend were introduced to pot by the friend's father— right in their home.

Does that make you fighting mad?

What about the home that exposes its children to 18,000 murders, 75,000 scenes of physical intimacy between unmarried partners, 75,000 commercials whose basic message is "Take a pill for a problem," and 66,000 commercials that say "Drink alcohol for fun." Those are the actual estimates of what a kid sees on television while growing up in the average American home.

The subtlety of this invasion is crafty, and the hypocrisy behind it is incredible. As one CBS executive remarked, "We have to remember, we're a guest in people's homes." One local station even has the audacity to use "For Kids' Sake" as its promotional slogan for this year.

It's an intrusion that slips into our homes like a cunning burglar, and parents indifferent to it are cultivating disaster for their kids.

Children become what they think about— it's a principle as certain as gravity. So what type of influence at home is worse— the father who brings home marijuana, or viewing the "average" amount of television?

Every album my kids play, every concert they attend, every television show they watch . . . each one is like a stepdad temporarily taking over my role of teacher, coach, and friend. Is it the kind of stand-in I want for myself?

Parents are the decision makers. The federal government won't help our kids avoid the worst influences. The city council won't. Our neighbors won't.

The responsibility is yours and mine.

So who cares?

You do.

I do.

How are we showing it?

☞

PART II

A Homeowner's Guide
to the Family Goldmine

This is how you can tell a father:
He's a man who will play with you
even though he has friends his own age to play with.

— from a Father's Day card
[© Hallmark Cards, Inc.]

—4—

The Light That's Nearest

You may beat us on the road,
but we'll get you at home.
— Sparky Anderson

TODAY I CAN HEAR A CRY— a desperate scream— from the kids growing up in our nation. They're crying for help!

The phone rings often in my home from parents calling with a desperate questions . . . searching for an answer, a place, a person to turn to for help with a "lost" teenager. As I write now I've just hung up from talking with a frustrated stepmother of a seventeen-year-old boy. She and the boy's father had tried psychiatrists, family

41

therapists, drugs, and several in-home techniques prescribed for handling rebellious children.

I knew the boy wasn't "born to be wild." But as I talked with her, she told how in his earlier years the boy had been shipped from one home to the other during the breakup of his parents' marriage. I wondered what would have happened if he had gotten more of his parents' love and attention back then.

"We've done everything," the stepmother said to me. "There's no hope."

What a tragedy! To realize "There's nothing else we can do" must be the toughest admission in any parent's life. But having known many people in this situation, I want to say, "YES, there is something more you can do!" Even in the desperate stage, I've seen good parents still willing to do anything, give anything, sacrifice anything to save their prized possession, their teenage child . . . *and many are finding success.*

LOOK OUT, MR. GALLUP!

IN THE PAST YEAR, *USA Today, Seventeen* magazine, *Source* magazine, and *Reader's Digest*

---

light \līt\ *n.* 1. As different from dark as a home is from a house. 2. The energy given off by a family enjoying each other; the radiance of Mom and Dad's love and approval; the aura of smiling and laughing together.

have published such statistical estimates as these:

• Of teenagers who drink one in ten will become an alcoholic. Three to five of the remaining nine will have serious drinking problems. There are three to five million teen alcoholics growing up in America today.

• Of all the fourteen-year-old girls alive today, forty percent will become pregnant by their nineteenth birthday.

• Sixty percent of all church-involved teenagers are sexually active.

• Eighty-four percent of all teenage boys believe that premarital sex is acceptable.

• Every year, 500,000 teenage girls in America have an abortion.

• More than 30,000 scenes of sexual intimacy aired on prime-time television last year, and 27,000 of them involved relationships outside marriage.

• Every seventy-eight seconds, a teenager attempts suicide in America.

• Sixty-six percent of American high school seniors have used illegal drugs.

• Sixty-seven percent of America's ninth-graders say they lied to their parents some time during the past twelve months.

These crazy numbers can depress a parent to death, and make a newlywed couple want to give up on having kids before they even get started.

But look out, Mr. Gallup! I've been doing a little research on my own, and I'd like to share with you encouraging evidence that kids are able, ready, and willing to go against their generation's trends— if parents do their part.

I spend each summer at our camps with five thousand kids from forty or so states. They range in age from eight to eighteen. With a staff-to-kid ratio of 1 to 3.5, my staff members and I get to know these kids well.

After surveying a thousand of them, I found that kids are still moldable lumps of clay. And they will receive whatever handprints give them the most attention. No matter what new theory the secular humanist would like to sell us, I believe children have an innate, genetically pro-grammed desire to be primarily molded by their mom and dad.

More than eighty percent of our camp's teenagers say they are against premarital sex. Ninety-two percent are against illegal drugs. The majority don't drink alcohol.

Why are these kids so different from their peers? Here's the kicker . . .

• Ninety-five percent of the boys indicate that their fathers regularly tell them "I love you." Seventy-nine percent of the fathers say it more than once a week, and sixty-two percent let those three magic words ring out every day.

• Ninety-eight percent of the girls say their mothers tell them regularly "I'm proud of you" or "You're doing a great job."

• Ninety-one percent of the kids say their parents play games with them.

• Ninety-four percent say their fathers attend their athletic events.

• Ninety-seven percent of the boys say they get hugs from their dads.

• One hundred percent of the girls say they get hugs from their moms or dads.

• Recalling their childhood, one hundred percent of the girls remember having stories read to them by their mothers. Eighty-five percent of the boys recall having stories read to them by their dads.

• Eighty-nine percent of the boys say their fathers have taken them fishing.

• One hundred percent of the girls say their parents have taken them to Sunday school.

I ONCE ASKED a friend, who was both an assistant coach of a professional football team and a successful businessman, what his goal in life was.

"Number one," he said, "is this: When my kids grow up, I want them to lead respectable, Christ-centered lives."

To that end he had made countless sacrifices in job opportunities and business ventures— some costing thousands of dollars— to keep his children in the same home, the same school, and the same church from year to year while they were growing up. For all his professional success, he hadn't lost sight of the importance of his family.

He never thought of himself as a super-hero— but that's what he is to his kids. They respect him not because he makes a lot of money or because he works with a football team or because he can "speak their language." They esteem him because in their family he's a true leader, giving them the one thing he can't buy for them— himself.

In pursuing his goal. this man has faced far tougher opposition— seductive mass media, humanistic public education, depraved music, the drug culture, materialism, and more— than was ever encountered by the football teams he's coached. But it wasn't hard for me, sitting across from him as we talked in his office, to make a long mental list of the characteristics that mark him as a Christlike man. His starting lineup includes . . .

> Love
> Enthusiasm
> Consistency
> Creativity
> Servanthood
> Discipline
> Prayer

These are the powerful weapons that make any mom and dad effective in defeating the villains of secular culture that attack our families and nation today.

You may not think of yourself as a superhero anymore than this man did. In fact you may feel your family life is in serious trouble . . . that your kids feel more like orphans at home than like the children of a hero. But there's hope. There are actually encouraging signs in the heat of the battle. When given an adult friend who will *really* love them (faults and all), and who will give them a consistent example of good behavior to follow, most teenagers really want to do the right thing.

As I'm around so many thousands of teenagers and their families, I'm also excited about two other facts that are still true in spite of all the problems kids face today.

First, there are so many parents who do a truly great job with their kids. They are accepting the problems as challenges, and meeting the challenges head-on with determination, self-sacrifice, and enthusiasm. They're being the heroes their kids need. The result is a number of kids who are more outstanding than any other generation of kids in history.

Second, the incredibly dangerous environment so many kids live in is actually bringing out the best in many of them. They're like a sapling in a dense, high forest that grows straight and tall as it competes for light. The tougher the challenge, the more many kids stand committed to the right principles they've been taught and shown. I am truly amazed at the number of teenagers today who take a mature, positive stand for Christian values and moral living.

CLOSE . . . AND CONSTANT

One clear and beautiful Ozark evening last summer, I was walking my youngest daughter home after an evening youth rally. A splendid display of stars spangled overhead, a gift to enjoy from our Creator.

As Courtney and I marveled at the heavenlies, perhaps ten thousand feet above us I saw a jet airplane cruising through the night, its lights dimly visible as it prepared to land at an airport fifty miles away.

"Courtney, see those lights?" I pointed overhead.

She leaned back further. "Yes, Daddy. What is it?"

"It's a jet, Sweetheart. See how dim those lights are?"

"You can barely see them!"

Capturing a teachable moment, I continued, "Those lights are very, very bright when the plane is on the ground, but the further you're away from them, the dimmer they get. See that brightest star right near the plane? That star is thousands of times brighter than our sun, but it is over ten million light years away, so it looks like a tiny dot in the sky."

"Wow, Dad, that's awesome!"

Just then a lightning bug only a few feet from us lit up brightly, almost like the startling flash of a camera. Just imagine— a lightning bug, whose tail measures only an eighth of an inch across, outshining an airplane's light that can illuminate a runway, or a star that could make the sun look like a flickering candle in comparison.

The principle I observed began to grip me with excitement as I related it to parenting.

For years now my kids have been exposed to negative peer pressure at school, anti-family music at their friends' houses, seductive messages on television commercials— a whole assortment of modern-day bad influences. Their world is full of it, all presented in the brightest trappings to light up the eyes of children of all ages. It all looks so appealing!

But I *can* shine *my* light before them . . . I can get my little flickering flame as close as possible to their eyes, and keep that baby turned on every waking hour.

My light— the steady beam of my biblical, old-fashioned, pro-family values— is small, and I can never give it the same seductive dazzle that the media fantasy-makers give their message. But I can always keep my light just a whisper away from those four precious pairs of eyes, as they look for leadership and direction.

YOUR BEST RECRUIT

Men and women in every career tend to give their best to their professions, and often— all too often— spare only leftovers for the family. Their children realize what they're getting— and when peers comes along and make them feel special by offering a beer or a joint or an enticing line of sexual allurement . . . guess where the child's allegiance goes?

Not long ago a successful collegiate coach

called me into his office to join his wife and
sixteen-year-old son for a "code-three" emergency
meeting about the family's quickly decaying relationships.

The coach was a busy man and gave seven-
day work weeks to recruiting and training his
world-class athletes. His wife was a divisional
director for her company, responsible for training
and supervising eighteen people.

The teenager was struggling. He wanted to
obey his parents— who had set commendable
guidelines for his social behavior— but when he
came home on time, all too often no one was there
to meet him. He felt he received no reinforcement
from home as he faced alone the peer pressure
from his social circles.

What could be done?

I encouraged the boy to continue honoring
and obeying his parents. His puppy-dog eyes will-
ingly gave away his deepest desire to comply. But
there was also a strain in his countenance. He
turned to his parents and pleaded with them to
give him the strength, the courage— the *relationship*— to fight the lonely battle that any good kid
must face in these difficult days for adolescents.

I thought of the great relationships the father
had with his players— all the time and trouble he
put into luring these blue-chip athletes to his West
Coast campus. Dinners out, expensive lodging,
impressive parties, numerous personal visits and
phone calls were all part of the process. He was
so successful. His players loved him.

Why couldn't he recruit his own son?

The father was open to instruction. We compared the value to his life of his son versus his players. He quickly agreed that on a scale of one to ten, his son was a ten and his athletes an eight or nine. Yet his son was being treated like a six, while the athletes received steady ten-and-a-half treatment.

We talked further at a later date. Eventually he left his coaching position to "recruit" his family. He sees now that he had taken for granted the son he loves so greatly. The boy, meanwhile, has turned away from some sources of negative peer influence.

Leaving that lucrative coaching position wasn't easy for the father. Choosing family over fame or fortune never is.

☞

—5—

Close the Zoo

As a man thinketh, so he is.
— Proverbs 23:7

A man is what he thinks about all day long.
— Ralph Waldo Emerson

A man's life is what his thoughts make of it.
— Marcus Aurelius

*It's not how many fish you caught with your son;
it's how much you laughed when your tent started leaking.*

THE ANIMALS in the Hong Kong Zoo were growing noticeably fatigued, unhealthy, and more edgy and testy with each other as the zoo grew in popularity and became more heavily visited by human observers. So, according to the account in *Newsweek,* the zoo's directors decided to give the animals time off by closing the gates to the public one day a week. The animals showed some improvement, but still there was more fighting and sickness than what seemed normal. Again the directors met, and decided to do what had never been done: Close the zoo two days every week. This time, results were dramatic. Health and playfulness were restored. The animals quit fighting. The directors were amazed.

There's a lesson there for parents. If your kids aren't acting like the maturing, lovable creatures they were meant to be . . . try closing the zoo.

If a crowd throwing peanuts can destabilize wild and noble beasts, think what's happening to the young people targeted by the arrows of pornography, violence, degradation and other dangers launched continuously from today's music and media.

I HAVE TO SAY I'M THE LUCKY ONE. Besides getting to be around my best teachers— the four kids who are spending their growing up years calling me Daddy— I have the privilege of raising kids for a living. Besides being around the thousands who come to our camps every summer, during the other seasons I travel frequently to youth rallies, school assemblies, and other events involving youth. Meanwhile, two blocks from where we live are twenty searching teenagers in a resident care home.

Taken together, these encounters afford me the opportunity to speak with many thousands of teenagers each year. The best moments for learning come when, from out of the crowds, the hurting few approach one by one, seeking emotional help with "Code Three" urgency.

Last weekend, for example, I spoke for ninety minutes to a group of several hundred teenagers at a leadership youth rally. It was followed by two and a half hours listening to a seventeen-year-old girl who already has had her third abortion and probably is headed for more.

This comprehensive exposure to kids has built up in me a mental computer bank with countless bits of information . . . problems and solutions . . . things that work and things that fail . . . knowledge of tears and laughter . . . of guilt and forgiveness . . . of frustrations and relief. It's all there. From it have come sound, deep, trustworthy patterns of counsel and teaching.

It all adds up to one overarching observation: A child becomes what he thinks about. And he thinks about what he sees and hears.

Kids are the way they are because of what they're exposed to, what they fill their minds with.

The human brain was created to be programmed through the senses. The human body was developed to respond to the information stored in the mind. If a child sees and hears often enough about the pleasure of sexual sin, then that is exactly what you can expect that child to do as soon as he or she is able. One plus one *always* equals two.

The family's social and economic background doesn't matter. Our family has enjoyed friendships

with families in poor, inner-city situations as well
as those who are among the nation's most
financially secure people— plus every range
between. The background doesn't make a
difference. What does make a difference is the
number of hours the zoo is left open.

THE SCREEN SCENE

Browsing through the weekly *TV Guide*
tonight exposed quickly the underlying script that
permeates the networks:

> "When it comes to love, everything is
> relative" *(the sales line below a photo of a
> thirteen-year-old boy and girl embracing).*

> "Her life belonged to one man until he was
> gone; now she must reclaim it for herself.
> MISTRESS, a secret life revealed" *(with an
> inset photo of a foreboding beauty in black
> negligee, lying across silk sheets).*

> "Smart, sexy, fearless— 200 years ago in
> this room a beauty was driven to a crime of
> passion. Tonight it's about to happen
> again."

> "Prom queen. Playboy centerfold. Movie
> star. Murder victim."

Sex. Passion. Seduction. Violence. Murder.
This year, the average teen will spend just over
twice as much time watching this immoral
programming as he does in the classroom.

It all adds up.

A child becomes what he thinks about.

He thinks about what he sees and hears.

We would never invite a murderer, a rapist, or a sexual pervert into our homes. But it is amazing how many of just such people we let in every day through television— on programs that make it all look so attractive to the growing, questioning mind of a child. It's pretty hard to expect a child to practice personal morality, use clean language, and stiff-arm any enticement to drug abuse when a twenty-five-inch screen constantly promotes the opposite behaviors.

MUSIC MAKERS, LIFE TAKERS

Resounding today from the radio stations kids listen to most are lyrics like the following, which take advantage of music's power to stick like glue to young minds:

> "Slide down to my knees, taste my sword"
>> *(Motley Crew, in the hit*
>> *"Tonight We Need a Lover")*

> "Cause when I go through her,
> it's just like a hot knife through butter"
>> *(Kiss, in the number one song*
>> *"You Better, You Bet")*

> "Squealing in passion as the rod of steel injects"
>> *(Judas Priest, in the*
>> *top forty song "Eat Me Alive")*

"My sister never made love
        to anyone else but me;
    incest is everything it is said to be"
            (Prince, in the solid-gold hit "Sister")

In an article in one teen magazine, Blacy
Lawless of the band W.A.S.P. says, "I like to drink
blood out of a skull and torture females on stage."
In another, Elvis Costello says, "Rock and Roll is
about sex and I'm here to corrupt the youth of
America."

Paul Rutherford of the music group "Frankie
Goes to Hollywood" once offered this opinion about
our children:

> Kids are really sophisticated now; they
> don't need to be sheltered. Little girls want
> to have sex. Teenagers and little boys, they
> all want to have sex. They do!

THIS PERVERTED, profane, degenerated blitz
against kids' minds has been the worst mass attack
ever made against our youth, an onslaught that
has raged through the eighties with weapons that
search the limits of depravity: Elton John singing
of girls having sex with girls in "All the Young Girls
Love Alice". . . Alice Cooper singing of sex with a
corpse in "Cold Ethyl". . . Gene Simpson of Kiss
talking in *Rock* magazine about "cycles and whips
. . . all the things little girls dream about". . . Pink
Floyd's song "Sheep," opening with the Twenty-
third Psalm then turning into blasphemy, echoing
so many other songs that portray Satan as nothing
to be feared and cast doubt on God's goodness.

Every day, one recent study shows, more than eighty-five percent of American teenagers listen to popular rock music for at least two hours. That adds up to at least 75,000 songs heard by each of these kids during his or her teenage years.

Meanwhile, a recent survey indicates that a parent spends an average of thirty to ninety seconds a day in one-on-one, face-to-face communication with his teenage child. If that child is getting hundreds of times more verbal input from rock and media stars . . . then guess whose behavior he'll copy?

Don't you think it's time to close the zoo?

SOMETHING BETTER

That dog Champ taught me another encouraging truth about this home of mine. If he had a dangerous chicken bone or sharp steak bone in his mouth, no act of Congress or California earthquake could make him give it up. But if I offered him a juicy piece of lean meat in the palm of my hand, then like any dog he'd drop that bone everytime.

Are your worried about the attraction some tantalizing but dangerous "bones" might hold to your kids? Then turn your home into a king's cut of prime rib to entice their tastebuds. Make life at home a celebration for them— a homecoming party every evening after school, and a holiday every weekend.

"The best way to make kids good," Oscar Wilde said, "is to keep them happy." Kids love to stay home when the home has parent leaders who make it the "funnest" place to be.

A picture I saw on a giant billboard years ago on Interstate 40 continues to stay in mind. A family of five was holding hands and walking together, all smiling. Big colorful letters read, "Get your good times together."

If you're concerned about all those quarters your children feed into video games, or the thousands of hours spent in front of the TV, or how hard it is to get everyone to sit down together for a family dinner because the kids can't wait to go out with their friends . . . then get your good times together, and the chances are excellent you'll find your family closer than ever in the years ahead.

I haven't listened to a secular radio station more than once or twice a year since our first baby was born. The record companies would go out of business if our family's habits were contagious enough. Hollywood would have the nation's highest unemployment rate if my kids set the trends.

But we play in our home like a bunch of monkeys. Our house is rowdy, fun, creative, exciting, crazy. Are we missing anything? Maybe. Are our kids sheltered? Maybe. But would I trade a hilarious, tense, competitive game of good old Monopoly to watch an hour of filth and violence on TV? No way.

Is there life after television?

You bet!

What else can a family do together? For starters, try a few of these:

Homemade carnivals in the living room, with prizes for the winner in each event: throwing darts at balloons, pitching pennies, tossing a hat on a broomstick, bobbing for apples.

Homemade miniature golf. Balloon volleyball over a king-size bed. Pillow fights.

Table games. Puzzles. Checkers. Charades. Coloring contests.

Making popcorn balls. Making caramel apples.

Leather crafts. Wood crafts.

Family baseball, football, volleyball (we always handicap the better athletes to keep the competition close). BB gun contests. Bow-and-arrows in the front yard popping balloons.

Shuffleboard. Go-cart racing. Rollerskating.

Window shopping. Scavenger hunts at the mall.

Spoil Mommy Day. Date Night with Dad. (I try to give each daughter a memorable date— as well as teach them how a girl should be treated by a guy— by opening the door for her, seating her, giving her preference, and talking about the love, admiration, and respect I have for their mom.)

Hunting trips. Fishing. Camping. Hiking. Horseback riding. Mountain climbing.

My kids still think I'm nuts for the day we packed a picnic basket with a white tablecloth, china, and candlesticks for breakfast at McDonald's.

LORD, MAKE ME CREATIVE!

The first requirement for being a creative, contagious family leader is to develop a happy heart. Maintaining a cheerful spirit is a constant challenge for me, as it is for most parents who face so many pressures both inside and outside the home. It dampens even the hearts that *want* to be happy. The solution that works best for me— and I believe it's the key to being admired by your kids as a happy person— is to be continually thankful for all you have.

I find the easiest days to be happy are when I wake up counting the thousands of blessings I have. "Thank You, Lord, for giving me life! . . . The sun is up again— what a fantastic day! Thank You, God . . . Thank You for Debbie Jo— what a super wife! . . . Thank You for such neat kids— for Jamie, Corky, Brady, and Cooper . . . And thank You for the forgiveness You've given me, and for the hope I have because I know You . . ." The smile begins to grow. The day brightens. And when the pressures come later in the day, I shoot thank-you arrows at them.

The second key to making your home a place for winning relationships is to take time every day to create fun and meaningful times together as a family. *Yes, you can do it.* As a professional football friend once said, "I'm through with all the negative self-talk I've been feeding myself about my not being creative. I'm going to ask God to make me creative, and to take the role of creative leadership in my family!" With the same attitude, you'll succeed. There are a million ways to be creative.

Early one Saturday morning the kids were up watching cartoons on TV. Debbie Jo had put in a tough week. While she slept, I tiptoed out of the bedroom and joined the kids. After about ten minutes of watching them mesmerized by an animated space movie, I was ready to make something happen.

We got a crazy idea, and within ten minutes it was in full bloom. Twelve feet of butcher paper, a handful of magic markers, four pint-sized children and an inartistic father were sprawled across the living room floor making a giant "We Love You, Mommy" banner. We each took a section and scribbled like crazy. Each letter became a unique work of personal art. I wish you could have seen Debbie Jo when she walked into her day of celebration!

Look back into your childhood for the good memories and you'll smile at the times your mom or dad did something crazy or fun to make the family laugh. We need more of that today.

Use your creativity not only to make home a fun place to be, but also to solve critical problems. I once was working closely with a seventeen-year-old boy who couldn't quit drinking— which, as is typical, led to lying and other problems. After a lot of fruitless discussions with him, I said, "I tell you what. Glenn, if you'll give up your booze for a year, I'll quit drinking soft drinks for a year." He knew how much I enjoy a Dr. Pepper on a hot day.

After six months, his habit was broken— and he felt so good about himself.

MORE FAMILY FUN

More ideas:

A "Love Bombardment" works especially well with children above eight years old. Have the family sit in a circle on the floor or around the table. Have each family member give an earnest, sincere compliment to a designated person in the circle. The person receiving the compliments can only listen and say "Thank you." After that person has been bombarded, go on to the next until everyone has been in the spotlight.

Make mealtimes a fun experience every day. Let Dad offer to take tomorrow's household chores for whoever contributes most to positive conversation over dinner.

Place a coin bank or jar in the center of the table, with the rule that anyone (including you) who makes a negative, grouchy, or critical remark must put in a quarter of his own money. At the end of a week or month, decide together on a worthy cause to give the "pot" to.

Clear the table after supper and have

everyone sit an equal distance apart from each other, with chin resting just above the tabletop, ready to blow. Place a Ping-Pong ball in the center of the table. Whoever lets the ball drop on either side of him gets put on kitchen clean-up crew for the night. (Keep going till everyone gets to help.)

Have a regular Family Night each week, and guard it from conflicts with anything else in everyone's schedule. Use the first one for family goal-setting. Everyone pitches in ideas about what he or she would like to see the family accomplish. (An important rule: Positive comments only.)

Clarify and organize your agreed upon goals, then write down specific ways to accomplish each one, including a measurable plan of evaluation.

An example:

Category:
OUR SPIRITUAL GROWTH AS A FAMILY

Goal #1: TO HAVE REGULAR FAMILY DEVOTIONS

Method of accomplishment:
> A five-minute devotional time together each morning before breakfast. Everyone will take turns being the leader.

Evaluation:
> "Excellent"—Seven days a week, everyone present.
> "Good"—At least four days a week, and no more than one absence.
> "Poor"—Less than four days a week, or more than one absence.

Goal #2: TO PRAY TOGETHER REGULARLY AS A FAMILY,
                     APART FROM MEALTIMES

Method of accomplishment:
    We all meet in Suzie's room at 9 P.M. for
    conversational prayer together.

Evaluation:
    (Same as for family devotions.)

Goal #3: TO MEMORIZE SCRIPTURE TOGETHER

Method of accomplishment:
    Memorize three verses weekly, learning and
    discussing them during our other times
    together.

Evaluation:
    "Excellent"—three verses learned per week.
    "Good"—two verses learned per week.
    "Poor"—only one verse (or none) learned per
    week.

    Use one Family Night each month to discuss,
reevaluate, and redirect your efforts on family
goals. You also can use these times to look
together at budgets, schedules, and vacation plans.
Another Family Night could be devoted to
brainstorming ideas for fun activities together.
After you list all the ideas mentioned, each person
can secretly rate them on paper, using a one-to-ten
rating scale. Collect the papers and decide to do
first the activities that get the highest score. If a
questionable activity (such as seeing an R-rated

movie) is suggested, just ask the question, "How would this fit into our family's spiritual or moral goals?"

I strongly encourage you, in your position of leadership in your family, to set and and seek to carry out family goals. An effective leader in any field always possesses two main qualities: (1) He knows where he is going; and (2) he lets others participate in his vision, and persuades them to go with him. Know where you want to go as a family, and— through genuine love and joy— get everyone else in your family to get there with you by defining and pursuing your goals.

A New Game

Usually the hardest times for me to do something creative and fun with my family— when I instead end up settling for a wasted evening in front of the tube— are when I'm trying too hard to dream up something new and different. But this year my two boys and I struck a gold mine. We've invented a game called "Climb and Rappel." Planning it took about half a day, but the game lasts all year!

The game is a takeoff of the little children's board game called "Chutes and Ladders," which has a game board made up of numbered squares interconnected by "ladders" that give you shortcuts going forward and "chutes" that send you back from where you've come. In our version, the game board represents a mountain, and the squares are labeled with numbers that correspond to a numbered list of special things to do with Daddy.

To make your own version of the game, start by creating a game board on a large piece of poster paper, marking it off with a hundred or so numbered squares. (You can model it after the game board shown at the end of this chapter; or, if you have access to a photocopier with enlarging capabilities, simply copy the model board.) Our family's design includes "climb" and "rappel" squares. When you land on a "climb" square, you jump up the mountain the designated number of spaces. When you hit a "rappel" square you go back down the distance indicated.

Place your finished board on the family room wall or on the refrigerator or in some other prominent place at home. Let each child in the family select a thumbtack or penny or magnet to serve as his token to move on the board.

Next, write your own numbered list of "creative parent/kid events"— several dozen things you and your kids like to do together. (For examples, see our family's list at the end of this chapter.) Have a special privilege reserved for when a player reaches the final square on the board.

It should take weeks or even months of fun to get there. Each day, or maybe three days a week, when the time comes for those golden minutes at home together, have your child roll the dice and move his token that number of spaces on the game board. Whatever number he or she lands on, go to the event list and do that event *together*.

We're playing our first game now— and my kids can't wait to come home from school each afternoon to roll the dice and see what we get to do together next.

CAUSE YOU WERE THERE

One beautiful spring day a few years ago I was tied up at the office until dark. My youngest "round and firm and fully packed" boy had his best friend over, and they romped and played G.I. Joe for hours. Boy, were they having fun!

I dragged into the house just before bedtime and picked up my happy boy, told him he was a champ, and bounced him like a basketball into the bed two or three times. It must have lasted all of ten seconds. Then it was time to brush his teeth, put on his P.J.'s, and hit the sack.

As I tucked him in, I asked, "What was the highlight of your day today, Cooper?" I thought I'd hear tall tales of soldiers at war. He looked me straight in the eye and said, "Getting bounced in the bed."

"Really?" I asked, half-shocked. "Why is that?"

He sunk in the truth: "Cause you were there, Daddy . . . cause you were there."

Honestly, taking time away from my family to write this book has been about the hardest thing I've ever done. It's like pulling teeth for me to get away from my growing-up buddies at night to spend time with pen and paper.

I'd rather be a daddy than anything I know.

Closing the zoo each day gives me lots of opportunities.

⌐⊷

Daddy/Kid events for the White family's "Climb & Rappel" Game

1. Go to Mr. B's for an ice cream cone with Daddy.
2. Identify five trees with Daddy.
3. Make homemade ice cream blizzard with favorite candy bar, with Daddy.
4. Play frisbee golf to Grandma's and back with Daddy.
5. Direct and videotape a family skit with Daddy.
6. Shoot three balloons in archery with Daddy.
7. Write an "I Love You" letter to an aunt or uncle, with Daddy.
8. Do the supper dishes with Daddy.
9. Go see Joey and Jeanie's new baby, with Daddy.
10. Play a game of "Sorry" with Daddy.
11. Take Chuck for a walk down by the lake with Daddy.
12. Do ten pull-ups with Daddy.
13. Make Papa's pancakes for breakfast, with Daddy.
14. Jog to Cougar Trails and back with Daddy.
15. Memorize two new verses in John 1 with Daddy.
16. Call G.G. and C.C. with Daddy.
17. Do a finger painting with Daddy.
18. Go for a free swim at S. of O. with Daddy.
19. Go with Daddy to McDonald's for french fries.
20. With help from Daddy, lead family devotion tomorrow on Romans 6:1-2.
21. Read Archie comics to Daddy.
22. Make a modeling clay dinosaur with Daddy.
23. Go with Daddy to see Kris and Diane's new baby.
24. Write an "I Love You" letter with Daddy to a former camp counselor or baby sitter.
25. Have a go-cart race with Daddy.
26. Shoot fifty points with BB gun, with Daddy.

27. Play a "Bozo" game with brother or sister and Daddy.
28. With Daddy's help, set up a family picture with everyone in costume.
29. Visit Pardner with Daddy, and tell her three nice things you see.
30. Make a batch of chocolate chip cookies, and go with Daddy to take half of them to a favorite neighbor family.
31. Play home-run derby (until ten home runs are hit) in the gym with Daddy.
32. Have a tallest building competition in building blocks with Daddy.
33. Go with Daddy to McDonald's for a hot fudge sundae.
34. Play four games of ski ball with Daddy.
35. Take a thirty-minute walk in the woods with Daddy.
36. Go with Daddy to see Brad and Debbie's new baby.
37. Go down and back on the monkey bars, with Daddy.
38. Play a game of Crazy-8 with Daddy.
39. Go with Daddy to visit Grandma and Pappy.
40. Have a field practice in baseball with a brother or sister and Daddy.
41. Go fishing with Daddy.
42. Tour K-4 with Daddy, and tell Pappy ten new things you see.
43. Hit fifty tennis balls with Daddy.
44. Do twenty push-ups with Daddy.
45. Go to Walmart with Daddy and buy something special.
46. Play nine holes of mini-golf with Daddy.
47. Shoot the 410 with Daddy.
48. Play catch-and-step-back with a tennis ball, with Daddy (play until you catch ten in a row).
49. Do a video production with Daddy for grandparents.

50.   Shoot five hidden balloons in the trees with BB gun, with Daddy.
51.   Go with Daddy to McDonald's for breakfast.
52.   Watch <u>Noah's Ark</u> or another Bible video with Daddy.
53.   Go to Christian bookstore with Daddy and buy a gift for Mom.
54.   Play soccer ball keep-away with Daddy.
55.   Call Pardner with Daddy, and talk for at least two minutes.
56.   Write a letter of appreciation to a teacher or Bob Abbott, with Daddy.
57.   Take Chuck on a walk to K-4, with Daddy.
58.   With Daddy's help, plan devotional for tomorrow morning.
59.   Do twenty seat-drops on the trampoline with Daddy.
60.   Go roller-skating with Daddy.
61.   (You make one up.)
62.   Take three photographs for scrapbook, with Daddy.
63.   Go to the park in Branson with Daddy.
64.   "Father Abraham" with Daddy.
65.   With volleyball, do throws and catches with Daddy.
66.   Make a cassette tape for G.G. and C.C. with Daddy.
67.   Shoot ten basketballs layups with Daddy.
68.   Shoot arrows from the balcony to the football field, with Daddy.
69.   Play hopscotch at Kanakomo with Daddy.
70.   With Daddy, make a crayon portrait of Mommie and write "I Love You" on it.
71.   Do ten front flips on the trampoline with Daddy.
72.   Dribble and shoot ten goals in soccer with Daddy.
73.   Tie four different rope knots with Daddy.
74.   Play checkers with Daddy.
75.   Set up a putt-putt game around the house and play with Daddy.
76.   Ride bikes in K-Dome with Daddy.
77.   Watch a Disney video with Daddy.

78. *Let Daddy bounce you on the trampoline.*
79. *(You make one up.)*
80. *Play around-the-world in basketball with Daddy.*
81. *Do twenty throws and catches with baseball and glove, with Daddy.*
82. *Go canoeing in Tarzanland with Daddy.*
83. *Set trot line in slough with Daddy.*
84. *Break balloons with bow and arrows, with Daddy.*
85. *Play shuffleboard with Daddy.*
86. *Paper airplane contest with Daddy—grand finale off the balcony.*
87. *Go to Christian bookstore with Daddy and buy a gift for Grandma.*
88. *Do twenty football throws and catches with Daddy.*
89. *Break three balloons with bow and arrows, with Daddy.*
90. *Write letter of appreciation to postmaster, sheriff, or police chief, with Daddy.*
91. *Play "Pig" in basketball with Daddy.*
92. *(You make one up.)*
93. *Go to Pardner's with Daddy and ride the wagon around the circle.*
94. *Do twenty baseball throws and catches with Daddy.*
95. *With Daddy, take two photographs for gifts to grandparents.*
96. *Do twenty football throws and catches with Daddy.*
97. *Play checkers with Daddy.*
98. *Tumble (Caw-Caw) in living room with Daddy.*
99. *Go fishing with Daddy.*
100. *Do twenty push-ups with Daddy.*

CLIMB & RAPPEL

TOP

100 | 99

96 | 97 | RAPPEL 5 spaces ▼ | 98

95 | 94 | 93 | 92 | 91 | 90

83 | 84 | RAPPEL 4 spaces ▼ | 85 | 86 | 87 | 88 | 89

82 | 81 | 80 | 79 | 78 | RAPPEL 2 spaces ▼ | ▲ CLIMB 2 spaces | 77

71 | 72 | 73 | RAPPEL 4 spaces ▼ | ▲ CLIMB 2 spaces | 74 | 75 | 76

70 | RAPPEL 7 spaces ▼ | 69 | 68 | 67 | 66 | 65 | 64

57 | 58 | 59 | 60 | 61 | ▲ CLIMB 1 space | 62 | 63

56 | 55 | ▲ CLIMB 4 spaces | 54 | 53 | 52 | 51 | 50

43 | 44 | 45 | 46 | RAPPEL 2 spaces ▼ | 47 | 48 | 49

42 | 41 | RAPPEL 2 spaces ▼ | 40 | ▲ CLIMB 3 spaces | 39 | 38 | 37

29 | 30 | 31 | 32 | 33 | 34 | 35 | 36

28 | ▲ CLIMB 4 spaces | 27 | 26 | 25 | 24 | RAPPEL 2 spaces ▼ | 23

16 | 17 | 18 | ▲ CLIMB 7 spaces | 19 | 20 | 21 | 22

15 | 14 | 13 | 12 | 11 | ▲ CLIMB 4 spaces | 10 | 9

START →

1 | 2 | 3 | 4 | 5 | 6 | 7 | 8

—6—

Test Yourself

I like to see a man proud of the place in which he lives.
I like to see a man live so that his place will be proud of him.
— Abraham Lincoln

Hands build a house; hearts build a home.

IN THE PAST TWELVE MONTHS I've had my wife, my closest employees, and my children evaluate my performance as a husband, a boss, and a dad. Boy, was I awakened! I didn't know so many blind spots were possible in a man with twenty-twenty vision, but it's been one of the most productive experiences of my life.

Anyone with responsibility— a corporate president, a coach, a committee leader, a parent— wants to know on occasion how he's doing. He can ask his peers, and get a fraction of the answer. He can ask his supervisors and get another partial picture.   But if he asks those who report to him, he'll get a real eye-opener!

That's why the suggested evaluation that takes up the last half of this chapter is for your school-age kids.   It's a "Relationship Inventory" to be completed candidly by each one to help you know how well you're doing as a parent.   The questions have been shaped by the input of a number of teenagers who've taken the test.

Make a copy of the Relationship Inventory for each of your children over five years old.   A child under age nine should be assisted by a trusted adult (other than his parents) in completing the inventory, and children ages nine to thirteen may also want that help.   A teenager will probably do best completing it alone.

Assure your child that there are no "wrong" answers, and that the more he opens up his heart to reveal his true feelings, the more helpful it will be to you.   Let your children know that you are humble and eager to learn.

COMPUTING YOUR SCORE

If possible, moms and dads should work together in reviewing the child's answers and computing the score.   After the inventory has been completed by the child . . .

test \tĕst\ *n.* 1. A trial that determines your true grit. 2. A set of questions whose answers reveal with depth and honesty.

Step 1. Add up all the numbers circled (you can use this space for figuring:)

Step 2. Divide the total you got in Step 1 by the number of questions the child answered (if he answered every question, that number is 20).

Step 3. Now round off the total from Step 2 to the nearest whole number, and mark the result on this scale:

1 2 3 4 5 6 7 8 9 10

| very poor | | very good |

If your score is high . . . keep showing your child love, encouragement, and support; keep being creative; and keep praying. Don't stop growing, but strive to get even better!

If your score is not as high as you would expect or like, I hope you'll really pull yourself into the content of this book and seek to expand on every constructive idea that it spurs in your mind. Be open to new directions in your family life, and redouble your energies spent in relationships at home.

If your score is quite low, I would encourage you also to consider getting a well-trained counselor to talk together with you and your child. (A caution here: Be sure it is someone dedicated to the authority of God's Word. A lot of the secular child psychology that is available and popular today is as destructive as it is expensive.)

Regardless of your score, be sure to carefully review your child's answers to each question, and talk about them together with the child, especially the questions on which you scored lowest. As you respond to touchy areas, don't kick over the beehive by being condemning or judgmental. Be thankful that your child has been open and honest about his disappointments in his relationship with you.

You're likely to be walking on tender ground as you review and discuss these answers . . . but consider this picture:

A farmer waits all winter for the warming spring days when he can get the plow out of his barn and break the soil for planting. The sharp, heavy steel of the plow is necessary to cut through the crust that has been hardening since the harvest months ago. The earth must be broken and ready before the seeds— little seeds packed with potential, representing the farmer's future livelihood— can be sown.

In every family there are layers of insensitivity . . . hardening crusts that hide crucial needs in a parent-child relationship. This inventory may well have been a sharp, cutting plow that cut through the crust and exposed those needs— perhaps painfully.

But say Welcome to springtime! With the soil broken and ready, it's time to plant seeds of love and commitment and encouragement, seeds that will bear an unimaginably good harvest when the growing season ends.

⚷

RELATIONSHIP INVENTORY

A Survey of Your Feelings about Your Dad and Mom

*H*OW TO DO IT: Each numbered statement below is an incomplete sentence. Below each statement— on each end of a scale of numbers— are two phrases that could be used to complete the sentence in two very different ways.

Think about how you would complete the sentence so that it reflects how you feel. <u>Circle the number on the scale that shows best where YOU are in your attitudes and evaluation.</u>
If you feel a question doesn't apply to your situation, skip it and go on to the next one.

1. In the eyes of my Dad, I see myself as . . .

1 2 3 4 5 6 7 8 9 10

| insignificant, unimportant | extremely valuable |

2. In the eyes of my Mom, I see myself as . . .

1 2 3 4 5 6 7 8 9 10

| insignificant, unimportant | extremely valuable |

3. In the eyes of others my age who know me, I see myself as . . .

1 2 3 4 5 6 7 8 9 10

| insignificant, unimportant | extremely valu- able |

4. If my father had something very important to do at his job, and at the same time I really needed him, I feel that typically he would . . .

1 2 3 4 5 6 7 8 9 10

| first take care of his work | drop every- thing to spend time with me |

5. I feel my Mom and Dad love each other . . .

1 2 3 4 5 6 7 8 9 10

| none at all | very, very very much |

6. The amount of love I feel in my heart from God is...

1 2 3 4 5 6 7 8 9 10

| nonexistent | extremely high |

7. The amount of love I feel in my heart for God is . . .

1 2 3 4 5 6 7 8 9 10

| nonexistent | extremely high |

8. After I do something special (such as create or build something very original, or score an especially good grade on a big test at school) and come home and tell about it, my Mom or Dad probably will . . .

9. When my Mom or Dad is occupied with something, and I interrupt to say I have an important question, usually she or he will . . .

10. It seems to me that, when it comes to his family or his other interests (such as his work, his friends, or his hobbies), my Dad's number one priority is . . .

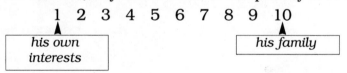

11. It seems to me that, when it comes to her family or her other interests (such as her work, her friends, or her hobbies), my Mom's number one priority is . . .

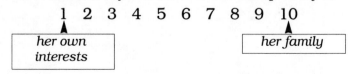

12. I feel as if my Dad knows the "real me" . . .

1 2 3 4 5 6 7 8 9 10

| *not at all* | | *very, very well* |

13. I feel as if my Mom knows the "real me" . . .

1 2 3 4 5 6 7 8 9 10

| *not at all* | | *very, very well* |

14. When I need advice and guidance, I go to one or both of my parents . . .

1 2 3 4 5 6 7 8 9 10

| *never* | | *always* |

15. When I am hurting, I go to one or both of my parents . . .

1 2 3 4 5 6 7 8 9 10

| *never* | | *always* |

16. Someday when I raise my own kids I will do it...

1 2 3 4 5 6 7 8 9 10

| *totally different from the way I was raised* | | *just like I was raised* |

17. I feel my overall relationship with my Dad is . . .

1 2 3 4 5 6 7 8 9 10

| *very distant* | | *very close* |

18. I feel my overall relationship with my Mom is . . .

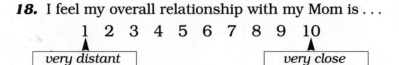

19. If I were to take this same survey a year from now, I would like to be able to rate my overall relationship with my Dad like this:

20. If I were to take this same survey a year from now, I would like to be able to rate my overall relationship with my Mom like this:

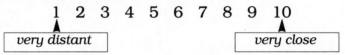

After thinking about these last two answers, write down here one or two creative ideas that you believe would help you achieve the relationship level you desire with your Mom, your Dad, or both:

And finally, write down two ways in which you believe your Mom or Dad (or both) could help you achieve that kind of relationship:

—7—

Unconditional Listening, Unconditional Love

It's hard to believe that a relationship can last when you've never seen one.
— Olivia Newton-John

I HAVE A PROBLEM," a teenager says (in word or action).

"What is it?" we ask.

"I want to run away," the teen says.

The typical adult response: "That's crazy! You'd never make it out there."

"Well, I'm going to do it anyway," he says. "I think I *can* make it."

Wanting to run away is not this teenager's problem. The wise parent— with listening ears, a loving heart, an understanding mind, and the foundation of a relationship built on trust— can find the real source of trouble.

"I have a problem."

"What is it?"

"I want to run away."

"What's wrong?"

"Nobody cares."

"I care. Can you tell me what you're feeling?"

"I just feel so confused."

"What about?"

"I feel so guilty."

"Can you tell me more about it? I really want to help you. I've been there— I've wrestled with guilt myself."

I'm not a professional counselor, but I've learned (Wow— have I learned!) that listening is the central ingredient in good counseling. The most valuable thirty minutes in my entire education process was spent in a small seminar with my colleague and great friend David Stone. He taught me an effective, simple method of listening, simple enough that it takes only thirty minutes to learn. Any patient parent can use it with a hurting child. It gives amazing results, especially when used with teenagers.

I've been swept off my feet to see the constructive process this method leads to in a teenager's moment of confusion. If I could encourage parents to learn and apply thoroughly only one communications technique with their kids, this would be it.

When your child comes to you seeking help with a serious problem or concern, and you want a way to tenderly but thoroughly discuss it, try this approach: Tell him you want to ask only three questions, but you would like to repeat them several times, and that each time you do you want him to give a different answer. Tell him your goal is simply to help him discover the proper solution and to work toward applying it.

For the method to work effectively you must follow three important ground rules.

First, you must provide an atmosphere of empathy— with your eyes, your facial expressions, and your words. The child needs to see and hear you saying, "I want to understand what you're going through. I care for you, and I'm eager to help you get to the heart of what's troubling you."

Second, don't jump to conclusions and give premature advice. The surface problem (drinking, fighting, curfew-breaking, disrespect, or whatever) is a result of the real problem that lies much deeper in the child's heart. Keep asking questions, and listen to uncover the real problem.

Third, don't condemn or criticize. Your

negative response will stop the process quicker than anything.

THE LEAD-OFF QUESTION in this method is *What's wrong?* or *What do you want?* You're finding out what's going on in the teenager's head.

Follow that with *What are you feeling?* Here you're discovering what's going on in his heart. In this second stage of uncovering emotions, you can "chase" the basic question with another to help identify more clearly the feeling. For example, you ask "How are you feeling?" and the child answers, "I feel sad." You could say, "What's the sadness?" His response might be, "I just feel so hurt, so rejected."

Next, ask *What are you doing about that problem?* or *What are you going to do about it?* When he answers, don't draw conclusions. Bite your tongue when you want to give advice. Instead, start over again with the lead-off question so you can sift down further to the real problem.

Be sure to kindly demand a different answer each go-round to each of the three questions. After a few minutes of patient questioning and active listening, you'll sense that the child truly sees an action he needs to take. At this advantageous moment you can say, "What do you need to do now to solve that problem?" Wait patiently for the answer. When it comes, ask, "Are you willing to do that? Will you come tell me how it's going after you do it?"

Learn to listen! Learn to ask questions! As

you help the teenager uncover the emotional mess that so often hides the real problem, you can help him commit to solving it.

Below are examples of how I've used the technique in counseling teens. (In each example, the teenager's words are in italics.)

ABORTION SCARS – *Polly*

"What's wrong?"

"I'm really hurting bad."

"How do you feel?"

"Terrible."

"What are you doing?"

"Talking to you."

"What's wrong?"

"I'm just so awful."

"How do you feel?"

"Sad."

"What's the sadness?"

"I don't know. Things are so bad, I cry every day."

"What are you doing?"

"I don't know what to do."

[Now the layers begin to peel off . . .]

"What's wrong?"

"I killed my baby. I killed him. I had an abortion last month and I feel so terrible. And he said that he loved me, but now he hates me. He said, 'I thought it would bring us closer together, but now . . .' "

[She begins to sob. I comfort her and wait patiently to proceed.]

"Polly, how are you feeling?"

"Terrible— so wrong."

"What are you doing?"

"I can't talk to anyone about it."

"No one?"

"Well, my parents won't listen. They're always mad at me and all they do is yell at me when I try to talk to them."

[The temptation is to stop here and and begin to give advice— for example, about not having premarital sex. But having sex is not her main problem. It's deeper than that. I find that many guys and girls who have been part of an abortion experience continue to be sexually active because there's something missing deep inside them.]

"What's wrong?"

"I just hate myself— I've hated myself for so long."

"How do you feel?"

"Mad at myself. Why can't I do what's right?"

"What are you doing?"

"I'm listening now." [She looks up at me.]

"What do you want, Polly?"

"I want to like myself."

"How do you feel?"

"Torn up inside."

"What are you doing?"

"I'm confused."

"What's wrong?"

"I'm not being me. I've turned into someone I hate."

"Who is the person you really want to be?"

"I don't know."

[I recognize the cop-out, and chase it.]

"Don't know, Polly, or just won't say?"

"Well, I don't want to get drunk and stuff."

"What are you doing to be the person you want to be?"

"I don't know what to do." [Another cop-out.]

"Don't know, or just won't do it?"

"Well . . ."

[At this point I open both my hands. I refer to my right hand as the real Polly that she wants to be, deep down inside, and to my left hand as the fake Polly that is making her so miserable.]

"Which of these do you really want?"

"I want to be the girl God wants me to be."

"What are you doing?"

"I don't know."

"Polly, what do you need to do to get what you want?"

"I need to give my life to Christ. I need to feel his love . . . get forgiven . . . you know, ask him into my life."

This went on for quite a while. I continued to refer to the right and left hand when she'd throw up cop-outs like "It's so hard." I kept her focusing on what she wanted more than anything else. Finally she found it!

ATTEMPTED SUICIDE – *Kathy*

"What do you want?"

"To be accepted."

"How do you feel?"

"Sad."

"What's the sadness?"

"Sorta lonesome, I guess."

"What are you doing?"

"It doesn't work. I've tried and nothing works."

"What do you want?"

"To gain my daddy's love."

"How do you feel?"

"I feel sad."

"You said that already. Can you think of a different answer?"

"Tired. Tired of trying."

"What are you doing?"

"I can't do anything. They find fault with everything I do."

"What do you want? What would really make you happy right now?"

"To make them happy."

"How do you feel?"

"Frustrated. I feel like a failure."

"What are you doing?"

"Nothing really."

"What do you want?"

"I want to be satisfied that I've done good."

"How do you feel?"

"Nobody notices when I do something right. They expect too much from me. They don't see the good things."

"What are you doing?"

"Praying."

"About what?"

"For strength to be able to talk to them again."

"What do you want?"

"I want to get along with my parents and have them as friends."

"How do you feel?"

"Frustrated, confused—you see, they're so condemning. They expect me to be perfect and when I make a mistake they come down really hard on me."

"What are you doing?"

"Trying to share with them."

"Trying?"

"It's hard."

"What do you want?"

"I know . . . "

"What do you need to do, Kathy?"

"Tell them . . ."

"Tell them what?"

"Let them know I appreciate them."

"How?"

"Thank them."

"How?"

"Do something."

"What?"

"Start all over."

"How?"

"I guess . . ."

"Guess?"

"I have to forget the past. [She cries softly.] Forgive them. I have to get rid of my negative attitude."

"How?"

"Focus on positive things."

At this point we made a list of all the positive qualities she found in her father, and I talked to her about how important it was to focus on the good qualities in a person you love. We prayed together to begin the forgiveness process, and she went away feeling a sense of hope.

I couldn't wait to spend time with her parents. The opportunity came a week later. After helping them realize a few things they were doing to injure their daughter's self-esteem, the family was ready to put things back together again.

I CAN'T SAY I LOVE YOU — *Bill*

After being away for three weeks with uplifting people in an atmosphere of fun and happiness, I came back to camp and encountered Bill, who at age fourteen faced a life of never-ending depression. He came to me with a scowl fixed firmly on his face.

"I've got a problem . . . I'm so down."

"What's wrong?"

"I don't know."

"Is it camp?"

"I don't think so."

"Is it your counselor?"

"Nah."

"Bill, I'm going to take you through a little process that I think might help you." [I carefully explain the three-question process, and he agrees to give it a try.] "What's wrong?"

"I'm just not excited about anything."

"How do you feel?"

"Confused."

"What's the confusion?"

"I just feel messed up inside."

"What are you doing?"

"Nothing. I don't know what to do."

"What's wrong?"

[Bill begins to frown. There is a long pause.]

"I just feel something missing— missing inside."

"How do you feel?"

"All empty."

"What's the emptiness?"

"I don't know. Kind of lonely, I guess."

"What are you doing?"

"Not much."

"What's wrong?"

"I'm not looking forward to seeing my parents, and I know I ought to be."

"How do you feel?"

"Lost."

"What are you doing?"

The Three Questions:

What's wrong? (or: What do you want?)
How are you feeling?
What are you doing about it? (or: What are
    you going to do about it?)

"What do you mean?"

"You say you feel lost; what are you doing to keep from feeling that way?"

"Hmmm . . ."

"What's wrong?"

"I can't tell them I love them."

How do you feel?"

"Sad."

"What's the sadness?"

"I want to tell them I love them. I just can't."

[Here again— as with Polly— is a cop-out that needs chasing.]

"Can't or won't?"

"Well . . . " [Long pause.]

"What's wrong?"

"I haven't told them I love them in so long." [He begins to cry.]

"How do you feel?"

"Really bad."

"What are you doing?"

"Nothing."

[It's time, I feel, to ask the pointed question.] "What do you need to do, Bill?"

"Write— I need to tell them I love them."

"When do you need to do it?"

"Today!"

"Will you?"

"Yes, I will." [A big smile appears on his face.]

"Will you come talk to me after you've written them?"

"Yes."

Bill took off excitedly to get his pen and paper.

The next day Bill came to me with another smile: "Wow," he said, "How can something so little affect you in such a big, big way?"

UNCONDITIONAL LOVE

I eagerly anticipated meeting Bill's parents when they were to visit him near the end of his camp session. When the day came, he proudly brought them over to me. It didn't take long to realize why he'd had such a hard time expressing his love to them. I told his parents what a fine boy he was and how much he had learned during his time at camp. "He needed to," his dad blurted out. I gulped.

The next day Bill won the fifty-yard dash in a camp track meet. Afterward I went over to where his parents were sitting in lawn chairs under a shade tree. "Did you see Bill's race?" I asked excitedly. "He won his entire division!"

"Well, he should have," his dad said. I gulped again.

The only compliment for Bill I got out of them in the three days we were together was, "Well, he's a good athlete."

Both Bill and Kathy had missed out on the full experience of unconditional parental love. They were part of the likely majority of kids today who feel the love and acceptance they receive from their parents is based on performance or appearance— "I love your beautiful eyes," "I love you because you made straight A's," "I love you because you scored twelve points in last night's game." When they don't feel they're meeting up to the expected standards, they feel as if the love is gone.

A very accomplished sixteen-year-old athlete came to me last summer after a somebody-notice-me suicide attempt. After a great deal of listening and digging into the heart of her insecurity problem, I found the roots of it embedded in the home of an over-demanding and temperamental parent. Two weeks later I carefully pointed out my observations to the parent, who protested, "But look at all her athletic accomplishments! She's the most motivated child in the family!"

"Yes sir," I agreed, "but do you know why she works so hard in her athletics?"

"No, not really," he replied.

"That's where she gets her pats on the back.

She feels the only time she's appreciated is when she succeeds in sports."

In contrast to the narrow demands of performance-based love, unconditional love is so creative, and so wide-ranging and rich in the response it breeds in the one being loved.

I'm the happy victim of seven cases of unconditional love. My parents really believe in me and hardly notice when I make a mistake. My wife has never demanded my performance for her

DAVE STEWART, a standout pitcher for nine years with the Los Angeles Dodgers, tells of a slump the team was going through during his last season there. The team had won only twice in ten games. Their frustration finally reached a peak in a game with Cincinnati, which they led six to nothing only to lose eight to six.

The post-game locker room was gloomy. Manager Tommy Lasorda entered and sat down beside his players. After much hesitation, Lasorda simply looked around at the defeated faces and asked, "What's wrong?" Wisely, he said nothing more.

After a long silence, one normally quiet player spoke up and expressed with heart-baring openness his own struggles and disappointments. Others began one by one to talk, venting months of pent-up frustrations. Several players broke down and cried.

Lasorda simply continued to listen.

The nightmare was over . . . and the transformed Dodgers went on to win eleven of their next thirteen games.

love. My four little children think they have the best daddy in the world, despite having front-row seats in which to view my shortcomings. This love has a powerful effect on me. First, it makes me so happy and fulfilled inside. Second, it puts a burning desire in my heart to please them in every way! I don't want to let them down. I'll do anything to do right by them.

Yesterday I had an eye-opening conversation with a girl who's a model of a well-rounded, responsible, moral teenager. She told me that her mom and dad communicated to her daily how proud they were of her and how much they respected her. Cindy told me she never wanted to disappoint such a great expression of love. "Even as I went away to college and lived on my own," she said, "I always tried to do the right thing. I couldn't stand the thought of letting my parents down. They always made me *feel* so loved."

I can't stress enough how much kids today need to see and hear and feel that unconditional love from their parents, over and over and over again. It's the pivotal need in their lives, and when it's received it forms the apex of every child's heart. It gives them the necessary strength and courage to face every pressure, day after day, for the rest of their lives.

I know in the depths of my heart that the committed love I enjoy from my parents reflects the unbreakable bond of my heavenly Father's love for me. I read in Romans 8:38-39 that nothing— absolutely nothing— can separate me from God's love in Christ Jesus our Lord. God had to go through a lot to back up that statement— and my parents had to go through a lot to back up their commitment as well.

My mom and dad have always lived each day to meet their children's needs, and I feel so fortunate to have grown up under such exceptional examples.

My mom is the total mother. She enjoyed meeting our needs to the maximum. When we grew up, a little inscription thumbtacked to the kitchen wall read, "The best way for a mother to have time to herself is at night when she does the dishes."

When we were young, Daddy read books to us until it seemed like all the print was read off the pages. He made the best Uncle Remus you ever heard. With his deep Mississippi accent, his sound effects and his imaginative gestures, he brought Brer Bear, Brer Rabbit, and Ol' Brer Fox right into our room.

At night he taught us to pray and gave us words of reassurance and encouragement to make our bed a secure place to snuggle into. As we grew up and our needs began to change, he changed to meet them. In the middle of his career, he sacrificed to take on ownership of a summer camp, so we could grow up in that environment.

I had many heartbreaks in my growing up years. Daddy was always there to pick me up as I fell. I'll never forget his love, acceptance, and words of wisdom the day I came home sobbing after finding out my best buddy got a starting position on the football team and I was to sit on the bench. Later, as a tiny noseguard at Southern Methodist University, I got killed Saturday after heartbreaking Saturday. Daddy was always there. I grew to depend on seeing his kind and encouraging face outside the locker room after the game. He didn't care about the score. He cared about me.

I think the key to the serving-love that made him best friends with my two brothers and me is the way he identified our unique needs (we're so different from each other!), and sought to meet them.

Brother Bob was a woodsman. Staring through a 30.06 Winchester scope at a ten-point whitetail buck was like Mardi Gras to Bob. He shot his first buck sitting in Daddy's lap at age nine. He shot his first moose, bear, duck, goose, and dove at various ages in various parts of the country, but always with the same hunting buddy.

Brother Bill was Daddy's most "interesting" project. Bill gave a taste of what was to come when he ran away on his tricycle. Dad knew how to get Bill through all the scrapes he got into over the years: "Stand by his side." "Be there to help him find success in his projects." "Keep him interested."

Well past retirement age, my dad continues to work daylight to dark, six and a half days a week, to help us have happy and successful lives.

HOW ABOUT THE KIDS IN YOUR LIFE? Do they really *feel* loved by you? Do they feel they can

depend on you to be there when they need you?
Or do they feel they have to measure up to your
expectations before receiving your approval?

THE MOST FAMOUS TEACHER of all time was
talking about how to become a great leader. His
view was typically revolutionary and to the point:
"If you want to be great, you must be servant of
all." His pupils remembered those famous words
when they later found Him kneeling before them
with a towel and bowl of water, washing their dirty
feet the night before He was killed.

The greatness Jesus Christ promised for
those who serve is reserved for those who give to
give. The folks who give to get are traders, not
givers, and they raise a family of traders to follow
them.

Take time today to write down the names of
your spouse and children, and beside each name
record some special deed you can do for each one.
That doesn't mean spoiling them . . . but simply
meeting their abundant needs for your time, your
expressions of value for them, your hugs, and
your encouragement.

☞

—8—

Which Way Are You Facing?

You can't plow a straight row looking backwards.
—Tom Johnson

*P*EANUTS OFTEN MAKES MY DAY. What's amazing about these cartoons is what's amazing about life. Maybe someday Charles Schulz will win the Nobel "family peace" prize for them.

A recent strip opened with Charlie Brown and Lucy, these two heroes of plain human wit, aboard a luxury ocean liner. They were strolling on deck, and in the background were sunbathers in lounge chairs.

With his typically simple facial expression,

Charlie says, "Lucy, some people's chairs face the back of the ship; they can only see where we've been."

He continues: "Some people's chairs face the side of the ship, and they can only see things as they go by.

"And some people's chairs face the ship's bow, and they see only what's ahead."

In the final frame he asks, "Lucy, which way is your chair facing today?"

A great question for Lucy— and for you and me as parents. Which way are *you* facing today?

Some parents like to pitch a tent and camp out on their children's past failures, like the seagulls that often follow ocean liners to scavenge the garbage dumped overboard. In anyone's life, the view backward includes some unattractive scenes. I've dumped some garbage of my own along the way. So have my kids, whose debris has sometimes been accompanied by my own mistakes.

The closeknit families I'm around aren't made up of perfect kids or perfect parents. But

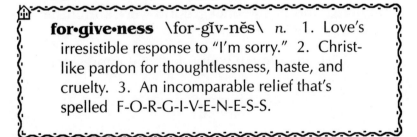

for·give·ness \for-gĭv-nĕs\ *n.* 1. Love's irresistible response to "I'm sorry." 2. Christlike pardon for thoughtlessness, haste, and cruelty. 3. An incomparable relief that's spelled F-O-R-G-I-V-E-N-E-S-S.

they do have this: *They're a team of professional forgivers.*

The father who comes to me for relief and says "You just don't know my son!" usually has a son who'll say to me, "You just don't know my dad!" I love to tell each of them that he's right, but that I know someone who knows them both and loves them anyway. In fact, the one who knows them best also loves them the most.

It's amazing to think about . . . God the Creator, who knows and sees everything behind and alongside and in front of our ship on our voyage through life, as we sail sometimes smoothly and sometimes with difficulty— our God is focused on our potential, and forgives everything— *everything*— about our past.

So I don't have to invent forgiveness. I don't have to produce it, as the sun produces light and heat. Instead, I just want to become a full moon, reflecting toward my kids the same attitude that God shines on me. My kids love it. I love it. My doctor loves it. I sleep good at night that way.

WRONG A LOT

IN ANOTHER *Peanuts* episode, Lucy is standing all alone in left field, mouth wide open, baseball glove thrust expectantly overhead. "I've got it!" she screams. In the second frame she calls out again, "I've got it!" Then a third time she proclaims to her teammates with commanding confidence, "I've got it!" Next we see the ball drop to the ground without even touching her glove.

Lucy stares at the ball, half-hidden in the grass. "I've been wrong a lot lately," she says.

I think she was trying to sum up my life. I've been wrong a LOT lately. Most of us have. We spend a lot of time thinking *I've got it,* only to watch the ball gather more grass stains at our feet.

It's the same with our kids, and always will be. So the question isn't how many balls will they drop, how many times will they disappoint us, how many letdowns will they go through . . . but rather, How will we respond?

Which way are you facing?

A STORY HAS BEEN HANDED DOWN through the ages of a generous king who liked to help the most promising entrepreneurs of his kingdom by loaning them large sums of money for their business projects. One young businessman with grandiose plans borrowed a million dollars from the king. The project turned out to be more consuming than the young man had dreamed, so he borrowed another million— and continued borrowing even more from his majesty. Some of the borrowed money he used to support the extravagant lifestyle he had adopted along the way.

Soon the end was near. Bills were long past due. The man's business was bankrupt, his pockets empty, his credit rating shattered. All his magnificent possessions were taken away, and he and his family moved in with kind neighbors. In humiliation and dread he awaited the day of reckoning before the king.

The summons came: His royal highness demanded to see this problem debtor.

Bowing before the ruler, the businessman pleaded in humble repentance for mercy. He promised that if his life was spared, he and his wife and children and someday his grandchildren and great grandchildren would all go to work in one of the king's factories for their entire lives, generation after generation, until the debt was repaid.

The king was moved with compassion. He decided to employ an outrageous grace heretofore unknown in the history of his own land or of any surrounding kingdom. He would set the young man free. He himself would cover the multimillion-dollar debt. He announced his decision, and dismissed the man to return to his family.

The sun seemed somehow brighter and the air so much sweeter as the young man skipped down the palace steps. *Now,* he thought, *by somehow pulling together a little cash, I can get a good start once again.*

Not far from the palace, he by chance encountered one of his former salesmen— who, the businessman quickly remembered, happened to owe him a thousand dollars, a debt that now was due. They exchanged greetings, the salesman complimenting the businessman for how well and refreshed he appeared. Then the businessman immediately inquired about the thousand dollars.

The salesman seemed to have trouble answering. The businessman's face reddened as the salesman spoke nervously about things being tight, and unexpected expenses at home. With sudden rage, the businessman grabbed the salesman's collar and promised to have him and his family jailed if the debt wasn't repaid the following day.

During a sleepless night, the salesman called in his friends to share in his misery. Early the next morning, knowing the king's kindness and generosity, they hurried to the palace and requested to see his majesty. When the audience was granted, they asked the king for a thousand-dollar loan to meet an urgent need, which they explained in full. They happened to mention as well the name of the salesman's creditor.

The king was furious. Before an hour had passed, he had the businessman arrested, questioned, and sentenced to life imprisonment.

WHEN I CONSIDER how often I have failed miserably as a parent, and contemplate the amazing grace I've been afforded by my heavenly Father, it really isn't difficult to forgive those tiny debts that are owned to me by one of my children or my wife. I can't forget the times I failed and had to ask God for mercy. I'll never forget:

> . . . the countless times I've come home after going somewhere with my family, and gone to my room alone, sometimes with

tears, realizing what a pitiful job I had done that day as a daddy.

. . . the times I raised my voice needlessly toward my wife.

. . . an unusually heated argument when I felt the urge to hit her. I'll be forever grateful I didn't yield to it. I pleaded for God's control, since I realized my self-control was still immature and lacking.

How many times I have failed to live out the sermons I preach to my kids!

With other failures in my personal life, I'm on a daily mental diet plan of thoughts of gratitude to my heavenly Father, who came to earth in the person of His Son, Jesus Christ, to pay off the enormous debt I've incurred here.

I spent the first two and a half decades of my life trying to climb the performance stepladder to gain acceptance from God. When I realized the ladder was too short, I appealed to His mercy to forgive my great debt. I began to base my acceptance from God on His grace alone. That's why I never get tired of Paul's words of security written to the early Christians living throughout Rome:

> For I am convinced that neither death, nor life, nor angels, nor principalities, nor things present, nor things to come, nor powers, nor height, nor depth, nor any other created thing shall be able to separate us from the love of God, which is in Christ Jesus our Lord. *(Romans 8:38-39)*

Recently a dear friend of mine died. He should have lived a few more years, but a fire that consumed his residence of many years left him despondent. He never really recovered the will to live after walking away with only his pajamas from the only place he and his kids had ever called home.

Shortly after the fire I telephoned my friend to console him in his grief. I asked him what was his greatest loss. He was a talented artist, so I thought he might describe a lost painting. Or perhaps the successful hunter in him would make him mention a favorite animal trophy destroyed in the blaze. He surprised me by saying he regretted most the loss of many spools of old family movies.

After reflection, I agree with his priorities. Beginning when I was a little boy, our family always spared a few dollars for filming home movies. They're a carnival to watch. Now my wife and I are regular users of videotape, but the fun involved with seeing the results is just the same— we roll on the floor laughing at Daddy's big nose and Mommy's crazy faces.

I've never met a mom or dad with grown children who felt they wasted money by taking too many pictures of their kids in the growing-up years.

Cameras don't blink, and these pictures of our family past show the good and the bad, the successes and the failures, the attractive and the not so attractive. That's an important difference between them and the pictures we store in our mind, the memories we keep of our children's past. Those memories can be edited— for free, and with computer speed—anytime you want to adopt God's forgiveness plan as your attitude toward your kids.

Again the apostle sums it up, this time in his "happy" epistle:

> One thing I do—forgetting what lies behind
> and reaching forward to what lies ahead, I
> press on toward the goal for the prize of the
> upward call of God in Christ Jesus.
> *(Philippians 3:13-14)*

The recipe for a good marriage always includes the ingredients of two good forgivers, and so does the recipe for a good parent-child relationship. I can't recall a teenager who loves and admires his mom and dad who has ever described to me a parent who holds a lot of grudges and reminds him of his past failures. As hard as I try . . . I can't think of even one!

But I have encountered many a boy or girl who displayed on the surface a smorgasbord of teen problems, and who told me about parents who reminded them of their faults. Though it always breaks my heart, it no longer surprises me, after I've spent time counseling a confused teenager, to then meet his parents and hear their judgmental, critical, unforgiving rhetoric about their son or daughter.

WHICH WAY are you facing?

If it's the wrong way, come back to your orphan at home. If you harbor the memories of his or her past failures in the family movies of your mind, take a trip to the cutting room tonight as you say your prayers. Wake up tomorrow and enjoy the beginning of a new relationship with a child who needs it so.

Give your kids the forgiveness God has given you. He never said, "Hey, change and measure up to my standards, and then I'll love you." He simply said, in dying on the cross, "I love you as you are. I've paid for your mistakes— past, present, and future. Now come and be my child. As your loving Daddy, I'll lead you in the right direction."

Just as He cleaned our slate, we should seek to wipe our children's slate clean every day.

☞

—9—

Take Me Fishing Again

As for man, his days are like grass.
As a flower of the field, so he flourishes.
When the wind passes over it, it is no more,
and its place acknowledges it no longer.
—Psalm 103:15-16

Each day is a lifetime in miniature.

HOW MUCH LONGER is Pardner going to live?"

When little Cooper asked the question tonight, the atmosphere inside our car became chilled and silent. My stomach felt hollow.

Pardner has never let us call her Grandma— she said she wasn't old enough to be a grandma. (She's now 93 years young.)

She's a born fisherman. She lived on the lake, and caught fish when the fishing guides couldn't get a bite. Going fishing with her was always fun . . . and always successful.

She didn't drink alcohol, but always kept a cold beer in the icebox, so that when the game warden dropped by for a visit he could have a "cold one." Her eyes would twinkle mischievously when he overlooked her freezer full of fresh catch, two or three times the daily limit.

Earlier tonight Pardner had called my family over to her house to give my two boys her fishing rods and tackle box. She knew her fishing days were over. My four kids, who so admire their great grandmom, couldn't understand why.

And I'll never understand why such a wonderful lady has to leave this planet where her kids and grandkids and greatgrandkids adore her. But I'm trying to be mature enough to leave the questions alone until the curtain between time and eternity is raised for me.

I wish I could have gone fishing with her more. I wish I could always hear again her classic East Texas Bonnie-and-Clyde stories of the depression days she lived through.

I wish I would have always shown more gratitude for her never exhausted striving to please her kin.

time \tīm\ *n.* 1. Something we're all given equal amounts of each day. 2. What must be invested now—or lost forever.

Funny how time slips away.

Funnier how we let it go unnoticed.

Funnier still how the only thing . . . *the only thing* . . . on earth that matters on nights like tonight is *family*. In this fragile moment the created things that surround us are empty of value. I couldn't care less about Pardner's will.

When the final song is playing, when the remaining grains of sand are so few in a loved one's hourglass of time . . . our life's priorities distill to purest value. And the certainty hits: You *never* spend enough time with your family.

How much longer is Pardner going to live? I don't know, little Cooper.

As I said my prayers tonight after tucking my foursome into bed, a renewed tenderness flowed through my mind. How much longer will any of them be with us?

Soon, Debbie Jo and I will have almost twenty years together in this house. I wish we could spend a hundred. I don't see her as much as I wish I did. We don't hold hands enough. There's so much about her childhood that I've never taken time to learn.

And Brady, Cooper, Jamie, Courtney . . . feels like just last Wednesday they were learning how to walk. Tomorrow (it seems) I'll wake up and they'll all be in college somewhere.

The more I'm with these precious little people who grace my life by calling me Daddy, the more I want to be with them even more. Getting enough time with your family is like trying to grab a tug-of-war rope that the other side is pulling swiftly through your hands. The harder you try, the more it burns.

I can't hold on to it . . . but I can cherish every minute of the time I have with them. I can savor every delicious Now between Now and Then. *Today* I can esteem my kids so highly that if I'm still here when one of their names is called on the roll up yonder, I'll be able to smile, and know I took every chance to let that son or daughter know, "You mean so very much to me."

Carving Out T-I-M-E

I HAD TO charter a private plane to come home last night so I could spend all of today with my family. It was worth every penny.

Last week I had to turn down a fantastic opportunity to speak to a prestigious group because little Courtney had a gymnastic meet scheduled that day. And business meetings can't happen on Saturday mornings, because that's when Brady plays soccer.

I'll meet when he can't play soccer anymore. I'll speak when she's too old for gymnastics.

A friend of mine owned several dozen small franchise businesses that really kept him hopping from city to city. He had been quite successful in his endeavors and wanted to pass his business expertise on to his son. When the boy was fourteen, the father called him into his study for a rare father-son meeting. He looked into his boy's eyes expectantly and asked, "What do you want to be when you're out on your own, son?"

"I don't know," he replied. "I just know I don't want to be as busy as you are."

The next day the father called a meeting with his partner and began drawing up the papers to sell all the franchise stores to the local managers. He kept only two employees in his restructured business— but he also kept his family.

He continues to be successful— very successful, in fact— in his business, but his priorities have changed greatly.

One of my favorite people is a father of two teenagers who lives in one of our largest cities. As his children began their critical teenage years, he was becoming a successful oil executive at a time when the oil industry was booming. He was being rewarded with responsibility, company ownership, and large financial gain. But even in the summer he left home before daylight to drive to his downtown office, and returned after dark to a lonely supper table.

After praying about his priorities, he quit his job, bought a small computer, and began his own business in his home. His business flopped and he lost countless thousands of dollars, but he gained a son, a daughter, and a wife. The love and respect they feel for their family leader today is immeasurable.

I read recently the story of the first-grade girl who asked her mother why her father brought home a briefcase full of papers every evening. Her mother explained, "Daddy has so much to do that he can't finish it all at the office."

"Why don't they just put him in a slower group?" she wondered.

The most haunting scenes to me in Thornton Wilder's classic play *Our Town* come when Emily is told in the graveyard by the angel that she can return to life to relive one day, but only one day. She decides she wants to return for her twelfth birthday. "Don't do it, Emily," the other townspeople in the graveyard tell her, but she decides to anyway. She wants to see Mama and Papa again.

The scene switches, and there she is, twelve years old, on the morning she remembers with such happiness. She comes down the stairs in a party dress, with her curls bouncing. But her mother is so busy making the cake that she can't stop long enough to really look at her. "Mama," Emily says, "Look at me. I'm the birthday girl!"

"Fine, birthday girl," Mama answers. "Sit down and have your breakfast."

Papa comes in, but he's so busy getting off to work that he never looks at her either. Her brother enters, also absorbed in his own endeavors.

Finally Emily calls out from center-stage, "Please, somebody, just look at me." Nobody does. Once more she turns to her mother. "Please,

Mama?" Again there's no response. Emily turns to the angel and says, "Take me away. I've forgotten what it was like to be human. Nobody looks at anybody. Nobody cares, do they?"

CHILDREN spell love T-I-M-E. Without consistent commitment of time, love can't be communicated.

Is it time to carefully reevaluate your daily schedule . . . and carve out more moments for your kids?

"How much longer is Pardner going to live?"

Pardner, I didn't want to take those fishing rods home tonight. Please take me fishing again.

☞

Part III

You're the Best

Catch your child in the act of doing something good . . .
and tell him about it.

— 10 —

Making Their Day —and More

I can live two months on one good compliment.
— Mark Twain

My dad believes in me.
— a teen, in acceptance speech
as new student council president

My parents think I'm stupid.
— Amy, a 16-year-old, after a suicide attempt

*During this period of self-doubt (ages twelve
to fifteen) the personality is often assaulted
and endangered beyond repair.*
— Dr. Urie Bronfenbrenner

I AM A MIRROR to my children. That's one of the most sobering thoughts I've ever come to grips with. They see themselves as I see them. If I am critical of them, they feel unworthy. If I am

127

positive and enthusiastic about them, they feel
valuable.

My sensitive wife sank this truth into my
mind one day when I was being overly critical of
one of my sons. "Honey," she said, "he wants your
approval so badly. He's always looking into your
eyes to see how well he's doing."

Most parents feel energized with love and
enthusiasm by a newborn family member, an
excitement that carries us through all the dirty
diapers, spilled milk, and sleepless nights. But by
the time that boy or girl reaches junior high age,
the mistakes caused by inexperience are no longer
little toddler messes— they instead can become
major family hassles. The boy or girl also has
picked up so many of Mom and Dad's negative
characteristics that a damper falls on the
relationship. At that point too many parents lose
the desire to be in their child's fan club any
longer, and they give up the All-American hopes
that motivated them before. But kids, especially
kids in today's world, never outgrow the need for
regular shots of praise that charge them into the
day with hope.

Kids will never stop trying for a father or
mother who thinks they're the greatest.

I FEEL SAFE in saying my number one job in

self·im·age \sĕlf-ĭm-ĭj\ *n.* 1. The concept
of me that I see through YOUR eyes. 2. "Mirror,
mirror, on the wall, who's the favorite of us
all?"

raising my children is the challenging task of helping them develop a healthy self-concept.

I've sifted through the complexities of countless teenagers' hearts during their times of intense crisis, and amazingly almost every tragic problem has the same root. The conversation may begin with talk about an abortion, drug addiction, or a rebellious attitude; but after a lot of time and empathy, when the layers of complex emotions are torn away, almost without fail a low self-image is uncovered.

Kids are so transparent when they realize the lack of direction in their lives. At a youth rally recently I spoke to kids gathered from several small towns in southern Missouri. As usual I enjoyed most the individual encounters with them after the assembly. The more teenagers I talked with that night, the more I heard about their having nothing to do after dark in these small towns (like most in America) except ride the loop in their parents' car, go parking, drink beer, and smoke dope. The blatant sin going on among teenagers in these situations is mind-boggling.

But one girl I met that night was different. Her standards were high. Her morals were sound. Her faith in Christ was solid. I asked her why she was different, and the next week she wrote to me her answer.

> I am proud to say I don't drink, smoke, etc., and that I am completely accepted by my peers. Whenever I am offered anything I firmly reply "No," and they accept it. I've found that some of my friends feel insecure or that they won't be accepted if they don't

go along. You really need to feel confident and sure about yourself so that you don't have to go along to be accepted. I credit all <u>confidence</u> I obtain now to my great parents. I don't know where I'd be without them building me up and telling me how much they love me, not for what I do, but for what I am. I am so happy that I don't do anything I don't want to and that I am not only accepted but respected for my views. I hope other teenagers will start respecting and liking themselves more, so that they can be happy with who they are without doing things they don't want to do.

Love,

Maria

P.S. Here's a quotation I read today: "Parents need to fill a child's bucket of self-esteem so high that the rest of the world can't poke enough holes in it to drain it dry."

A healthy self-image is a balance of confidence, humility, and security. More than ninety percent of the job of instilling it is

What is your child like?
Who is he?
He is not as he sees himself.
He is not as you see him either.
Your child is AS HE SEES HIMSELF IN YOUR EYES.

assigned to parents.
If you haven't started
yet, the time to begin is
now, no matter what
age your child is.

Here are some
simple ways to help
make it happen:

1. Say "I love
    you" every day,
    both in words
    and actions.
    *(Builds
    confidence.)*

> *The giant oak sleeps in the acorn . . . Grandma's apple pie rests patiently in the appleseed . . . and within every young soul is a great vision for life, awaiting nurture from the parent who continuously dreams expectantly —and who lovingly communicates that dream to the child again and again.*

2. Say "You're very valuable to God and to me" every day, both in words and in actions.
    (Builds confidence.)

3. On a regular basis, offer *loads* of encouragement, focusing especially on areas of heart and character development, rather than physical appearance, athletic ability and so on.
    (Builds security.)

4. Memorize Scripture verses together, and review and discuss them every day.
    (Builds confidence and humility.)

5. Go to God in prayer together every day.
    (Builds confidence and humility.)

6. When you sin, hurt, or offend, ask for

both God's forgiveness and the child's.
(By example, builds humility.)

7. Consistently and with joy, serve and submit to your husband or wife, as well as serving your children.
(By example, builds humility.)

8. Regularly in both words and actions, communicate your commitment to your husband or wife, as well as to the child.
(Builds security.)

9. When punishment is required, punish the sin but love the child.
(Builds security.)

10. By both example and instruction, teach the child to talk positively about himself and others.
(Builds confidence.)

11. Provide the child with continual opportunities for success experiences.
(Builds confidence.)

Though these guidelines are simple, they are time-consuming. But it takes only a moment to rip apart this fragile aspect of a child's inner being. Here are some common ways parents do it:

1. Being too proud to say "I'm sorry."

2. Being too proud to submit to and serve one another or their kids.

3. Finding humor in making cutting remarks

> **A** *child with a healthy self-image is one who:*
> *. . . understands his secure position in Christ.*
> *. . . finds great favor in his parents' eyes.*
> *. . . realizes the importance of obedience,*
> *   integrity, and honor.*
> *. . . is given opportunities for success*
> *   experiences.*

to a child, or using such remarks when correcting or disciplining.

4. Offering encouragement only for such externals as looks, clothing, hair style, and athletic skills.

5. Comparing their own successes with their child's failures.

6. Letting their child "get away" with disobedience or ungratefulness.

7. Laughing at their child's failures.

8. Letting a child have his way when his motives are wrong.

9. Punishing too harshly.

10. Making behavior demands of their children that are inconsistent with their own example.

To give you a window into adolescent hearts that have suffered from the parental destruction of self-image, here are quotes from a few letters I've received from teens, all in the past year:

If I have ever had a question, I'm scared to ask it at home. I hate being yelled at. Now if you were in my shoes, wouldn't you hate yourself too? Well, I do. I hate life.

Amy

I don't like my dad very much. Not once has he really hugged me. Rarely has he told me he loves me. I feel so awful because I can't ever run to my dad and have him make things okay. I can never cry on my dad's shoulder. Not once has he ever said, "Julie, things will be okay." I want so badly to scream and let out all of this hurt. I feel so alone.

Julie

You told me you were proud of me. Thanks for making my day. No one ever said that to me before. My dad used to tell me I would never amount to anything. It took a long time to get over that.

Andy

My mom hurts me so bad. She says one of the reasons she doesn't like me is because I'm dumb, and she says I have never been a healthy kid. My grades are six F's and one D. Maybe I am stupid like my mom tells me.

Sharon

AN OLD STORY is told of a smart-aleck ten-year-old who came to a wise old man and wanted to make him stumble. The boy had a baby bird in his palm.

Into a face highlighted with wisdom's wrinkles and crowned with gray hair, the boy poked his question: "Sir, is this bird in my hand dead or alive? Tell me, if you are so wise."

> *If a child lives with criticism he learns to condemn.*
>
> *If a child lives with tolerance he learns to be patient.*
>
> *If a child lives with security he learns to have faith.*
>
> *If a child lives with fairness he learns justice.*
>
> *If a child lives with approval he learns to like himself.*

Assured that the bird was alive, the old sage knew that if he said it was, the insensitive boy would crush it to death in his hand before opening his palm. If he said the bird was dead, the boy would let it fly away in freedom, but still mock him for his error.

Looking steadily into the boy's cold eyes, the man said softly, "Son, it is as you will it."

So it is with us. In our hands lie the fragile egos of our children, and the power to either crush them . . . or let them soar.

The layers beneath the teen crisis:

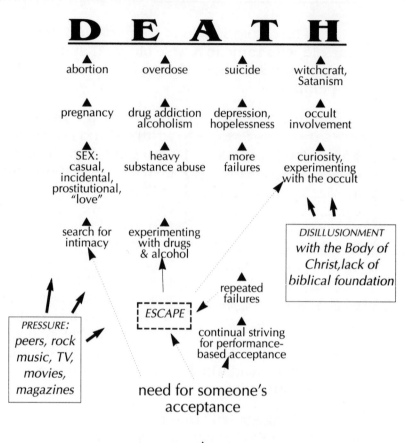

D E A T H

▲ abortion	▲ overdose	▲ suicide	▲ witchcraft, Satanism
▲ pregnancy	▲ drug addiction alcoholism	▲ depression, hopelessness	▲ occult involvement
▲ SEX: casual, incidental, prostitutional, "love"	▲ heavy substance abuse	▲ more failures	▲ curiosity, experimenting with the occult
▲ search for intimacy	experimenting with drugs & alcohol	▲ repeated failures	DISILLUSIONMENT *with the Body of Christ, lack of biblical foundation*

ESCAPE

PRESSURE: *peers, rock music, TV, movies, magazines*

continual striving for performance-based acceptance

need for someone's acceptance

▲

LOW SELF ESTEEM

▲

The VOID at HOME

MISSING EXPERIENCES:

• Reality of God's love, through a personal relationship with Jesus Christ

•Reality of parents's love, consistently demonstrated in action and attitude

—11—

Help Them Dream, Help Them Build

Anyone can count the seeds in an apple,
but only God can count the apples in a seed.

It's not to fear that a child's life ends in early death . . .
but that it never really begins.

RECENTLY, AFTER ANOTHER of the exhausting daily jogs that hurt worse with every added candle on my birthday cake, I plodded up that long, last hill, knowing that in all rights an ambulance and respirator should be at the top to meet me. At the last curve near the top, I passed a large, gushing fountain I built the second year I went to work for my father. Beside it was a twenty-foot sugar maple I planted at the same time, fifteen years ago. As my eyes met the breathtaking yellow and

137

orange leaves, I forgot for an instant how tired I
was. My face lifted. A fresh shot of adrenaline
gushed through my veins and pushed the lactic
acid out of my cramping muscles.

My mind raced back . . . to that exciting
time when I was a wet-behind-the-ears college
graduate. I felt the warmth of fulfillment as I
recalled the winter day when I dug the young
maple from the woods with a shovel. And I
remembered getting up at dawn, day after day, for
a trip in our two-ton truck deep into the hills of
Arkansas to load by hand the thousands of sand
rock that would form the fountain's veneer.

My daddy didn't want to spend the $6,000
the fountain cost, though I did. He was the boss,
and I was only a rookie in a business he had
slaved thirty years to establish. But he let me
build the fountain.

I didn't do everything right. During one
crisis in the field engineering stage, as we poured
concrete and worked like crazy as it set up, Daddy
sweated and worked shoulder-to-shoulder with
me so I wouldn't fail.

Daddy taught me how to dream dreams. He
dreamed with me. He helped my dreams come
true. The fountain and that sugar maple are
monuments not to the kid who built and planted
them, but to the daddy who encouraged him along
the way. Daddy taught me how to have a vision

vi•sion \vĭ-zhŭn\ *n.* 1. A dream (and more)
about happily ever after.

. . . to create an idea and help that idea mature into full bloom.

Too many kids in America weren't taught that. They feel like failures. That's why they kill themselves with drugs and bullets and alcohol and thoughtless sex.

Most of these kids have at least one "successful" parent— someone who can put together the big deal. Someone who manages the business well and wins approval from the board of directors. Someone who can make the home happen— the meals, the bills, the shopping, the cleaning, the lawnwork, the repairs. Someone who excels at certain hobbies. Someone who can buy and wrap presents. When it all succeeds, we feel good inside, strengthened. Our self-image is lifted. But is something— someone?— getting overlooked?

A FRIEND OF MINE came from a home that knew how to make children feel loved. Her parents adopted two children, ages six and seven, whose mother was a prostitute. The children never knew a father. They literally spent their first few years living in a doghouse with a dog. All they could do verbally was grunt, growl, and bark. Their IQ's were measured at 37. The diagnosis was hopeless: "Permanent institutional cases. . . . They'll never be normal."

But they began to discover love. Each day they'd hear over and over again the words "I love you." They were overwhelmed with hugs and pats on the back.

On the day they learned to say the word *love*, they ran in and out of their play room repeating it countless times. Their first spoken sentence was "I love you," addressed to their mommy and daddy.

In a year's time they were able to read and discuss a daily newspaper.

SHOWCASE

MY LAST BIRTHDAY was the best yet. At 7 A.M. all four of my kids burst into my room singing

The life of one of the most respected heroines in our nation's history has a fascinating but little-known story behind it.

In a basement cell of an old New England psychiatric home late in the last century, an unresponsive, cataleptic, schizophrenic patient lay curled in a ball on a bench. She had been written off as incurable. She spoke not a word and would not move from her fetal position.

A housemaid passed her cell each day on her rounds. She would shove a plate of food under the door to the "hopeless" girl inside. Before leaving, she also would gently nudge the girl with the end of her mop handle. As she communicated with the girl day after day with the only means she had, she was saying, "Someone out here cares for you. You haven't been forgotten."

As the weeks and months went by, the girl

"Happy Birthday" in four different keys. The first to reach the bed where I was still half asleep was Cooper, the youngest, wearing his famous smile. "Happy birthday, Daddy!" he blurted out as he dove into my arms and presented me with my first present of the day. The little lump was wrapped in paper that had been half-folded, half-wadded around it. A piece of secondhand ribbon was taped on top, the ends hanging down limply like a girl's pigtails on a hot summer day.

"Thanks, Cooper," I said with as much enthusiasm and sincerity as I could muster.

began to come out of her ball. She began to receive the food with her hands. Soon she was sitting up. As time went by, she began to communicate with the housekeeper, and eventually was totally cured.

Later the director of the home was confronted by a desperate man from Tuscumbia, Alabama. He requested someone who could work with a blind, deaf mute, a girl who also had received the "hopeless" label. The director introduced the man to the miraculously cured girl who had occupied the basement cell—Annie Sullivan—and thus began her historic work with Helen Keller.

Love meets practical needs any way it can—even if all you have to work with is a mop handle! Although our children's attitudes and actions may sometimes be so disappointing as to make the situation seem hopeless, the parent who continues to serve them will be rewarded.

☞

Inside the wrapping paper I found that the present itself was another piece of paper, tightly wadded up.

"Uh, what is it, Little Buddy?"

"It's a hand grenade, Daddy. Do you like it?"

Sensing his search for assurance, I went off like a New Year's celebration. "You bet I do! Best hand grenade I've ever seen! Did you make it all by yourself?"

"Yes sir, all by myself!"

He's been making me things ever since. I make a trophy of each one.

There are times when a parent must thoughtfully and firmly punish a child for the negatives. But ten times more often (at least) are the moments you can praise a child for the masterpieces that express his creative talents.

Our refrigerator is a showcase for school drawings. My office bulletin board has pictures and love letters from the hands of my children in their moments of inspiration.

GO FOR THE HEISMANN

AFTER AN EXCITING September college football telecast, the on-the-field announcer found the happy parents of the quarterback who had just led his team to a spectacular upset. The parents fairly consumed the ABC microphone with expressions of pride for their son as they answered the opening how-do-you-feel question.

"Do you think he deserves the Heismann Trophy?" the commentator continued, shouting over the crowd's victory cheers.

"Of course he does," the father answered with a smile that filled my heart with understanding. "My son was *made* for the Heismann."

That's it, I thought to myself. *That's the secret to successful parenting.*

The Scripture verse says, "Train up a child in the way he should go . . ."

And where should he go?

Go for the Heismann Trophy. Go for the best.

Not for a perishable gold statue poised for dust-gathering in a glass case . . . not for being the best player in college football . . . but for being the best in life. The best he or she can be.

Do you believe your child was *made* for this . . . to be the *best?*

☞

TODAY'S TEENS tell how their parents have both succeeded and failed in meeting their needs for encouragement:

Q. What specific things do your parents do that make you feel good about yourself?

"Back me up in all I do, discuss problems or joys with me, encourage me in all I do, trust me with a lot of things, spend time with me, share their life and love!"

"My mom and dad will take time out of their schedules to meet my needs or to be with me. They tell me 'I love you' a lot, or 'You're a great kid' or 'I'm proud of you.' They are open with me and will talk to me when I ask them to. They trust me with a lot and give me a lot of freedom to do my own things."

"What makes me feel the best is that they trust me so much. They give me a lot of mature responsibility and they trust me with all their hearts. I love them so much for that trust."

"They always tell me that they are proud of me— no matter what I do. I've always had a problem with my grades (I'm just not a good student), but Daddy always tells me that grades are important but that communication with people is more important, and I believe that."

"I have a very special relationship with both of my parents. I talk to them about everything. Especially my mom. She's my best friend."

"They love me."

"They make me feel good about myself by praying with me. They encourage me a lot. They tell me that they love me."

"They congratulate me even if I fail. They try and lift my spirits."

"They tell me what God is doing in their lives, and they ask me for my advice."

Q. What do your parents do that makes you feel discouraged?

"Hurt each other."

"They get mad at each other and take it out on me."

"All in all, my parents know that I am a good, responsible kid. I never do big things to get in trouble for, so they pick on little things. Colossians 3:21 says, 'Fathers (parents), don't scold your children so much that they become discouraged and quit trying.' Which is so often how I feel. I wanted to give up so many times, and if it weren't for my relationship with Jesus Himself it would have been so easy for me to give up. My sister, on the other hand, is a total

opposite. She is kind of a rebel and she gets
away with anything, which makes me resentful."

"They are perfectionists and point out
everything I do wrong. Sometimes they push
me too much in activities."

"They don't remember to also tell me positive
things when they are telling me things I need to
work on."

"FIGHT!!! Every morning, afternoon, and night."

"As he gets older, my dad doesn't seem to want
to listen or to want to talk as much, although he
is a great resource to tap into."

"I want to give up. I have nothing here. I barely
have a mother and father who appreciate me,
love me, and say they're proud of me. Nothing
matters anymore. I might as well crawl in a
corner of the world and die. God doesn't even
want me now. I'll probably get used to Hell. I've
lived in hell for almost 20 years now, so what's
an eternity?"

**Q. What is one positive thing your parents
have done that you'll always remember
most?**

"Told me about Jesus."

"My parents told me about Jesus and led me to
accept Him as my Savior."

"They spanked me for seeing my brother do

something and not admitting it. They told me if I saw something being done against the rules and I was aware of it and didn't do anything I was guilty too. I'll never forget that wonderful lesson."

"The most positive thing is when they sent me to camp. It changed my life <u>so</u> much. It's given me friends, real ones! Of course, it led me to my best friend—Jesus."

"Dad drove two hours out of his way to look at a puppy. My mom picked me up from school and took me to lunch and shopping all day."

"When I was 7 my dad took me on our 'date' on Valentine's Day. We went to a concert of our favorite group and I got to stay out late."

"My dad promised to take me kite-flying. He accidentally cut his arm and went to the hospital. He still took me kite-flying when he got back."

"One time my dad and step-mother drove 2 hours just to watch a basketball game I was cheering at."

Q. What is one negative thing your parents have done that will be hardest to forget?

"They punished me for something I didn't do."

"They don't listen and I have to totally get their attention. I feel like I'm not even there and that they aren't paying any attention to me. They don't tell me some of their problems just so I won't be worried with them. I would rather help them and know when they feel upset or discouraged, so I can encourage."

Q. What special things do your parents do to strengthen your relationship with them?

"Go to church and spend Sundays together with the entire family."

"Dad takes me out once a year for my birthday to talk about my next year."

"Pray for and with me."

"They are very gentle as they tell me or ask me things."

"When they know they are wrong (hardly ever), they apologize."

"Plan their schedules around the kids."

"They let me talk to them about the opposite sex."

"They understand my weaknesses. They NEVER compare me with my sister! They are so humble.

⊙┳

—12—

A
Cheerleader

Go! . . . Go! . . . GO!

TODAY SHE'S MY WIFE. Yesterday she was the enthusiastic girl with long, frosted pigtails that bounced as she ran . . . a cheerleader par excellence.

With three years of cheerleading experience in junior high, four in high school, and four in college, plus her fifteen-year directorship of a cheerleading camp, she's certainly earned the right to be counted in the professional ranks.

To her, cheerleading was a sincere expression of excitement for her team. Sometimes— as I watched her racing up and down the sidelines encouraging the SMU athletes, or making the call well before the man in black and white did— I wondered if she didn't put on that red and blue

149

skirt-and-sweater uniform just so she could be the person closest to the action on the field.

Debbie Jo has always been a cheerleader. And she's still one today. Now that her megaphone is in storage, her style is that of a quiet, consistent encourager. She applauds, consoles, encourages.

She reminds me so much of what is perhaps the greatest story the greatest teacher ever told. In Mark 4, Jesus tells His disciples about the farmer who cast his seeds to the wind. Some of them fell where there was no soil (they didn't take root), some on rocky, shallow soil (where they sprang up quickly but withered away just as fast), some among thorny vines (choked out after sprouting), and some among good, deep soil (they grew like crazy— and before long produced new seed for future generations).

In her commitment as a cheerleader-mom, Debbie Jo consistently sows seeds. Sometimes the kids' hearts are hard and the seeds don't sprout. But she continues sowing. Some days her good deeds and good words may go unnoticed, or maybe noticed but not appreciated. She keeps the seeds coming. There are days when her teaching is choked out by the misleading secular influences at school, in textbooks, or from the media. She keeps sowing the seeds.

cheer·lead·er \chēr-lē-dĕr\ *n.* 1. The Mom or Dad who continually gives encouragement from the sidelines. 2. The parent who truly prays without ceasing for each child.

Every now and then, the moment is ripe, the soil deep and fertile with humility. Jamie breaks her wrist in volleyball, Courtney tears ligaments in her ankle in gymnastics, Brady sits on the bench in soccer. The teachable moment is present. The seeds fall into open hearts.

Debbie Jo's seeds are always in the air. "Good job, Jamie!" "Brady, I'm proud of you." "Cooper, that was really a super paper you turned in!" "Courtney, I never did it that well when I was growing up!"

A hug, a pat on the back, a tear wiped lovingly from a sad face . . . seeds.

Walking her kids all the way to the bus stop.

Regularly planned special nights out for each child, one-on-one with Mom.

Personal evening Bible studies with the girls.

Attending every school program and athletic event that the kids are in (making for a full calendar, with four children).

Going to the game even when her child is injured and sitting on the bench.

Making lunches every day.

Helping clean up the mess while encouraging the embarrassed child who made it.

Planning and celebrating a special birthday party with customized cake and decorations *every* year for *every* child.

Creatively giving a special touch to every

Christmas, Valentine's Day, Easter, and Thanksgiving.

Always being available to help with homework.

Letting her kids see her unfailing encouragement and support for her husband.

Seeds.

Some end up in the rocks or in the weeds. But any good cheerleader-mom knows that the more seeds she sows, the more that will find the perfect, fertile soil, and grow.

My prediction is that when this cheerleader someday becomes a grandmother, her four kids are going to be spreading seeds in the same lavish way . . . and Debbie Jo's harvest will be multiplied.

I MET ANOTHER CHEERLEADER-MOM last summer. With her was her seventeen-year-old son. "Joe," she said, "this is my wonderful son. He's tall because his heart is so big it just keeps pushing him higher and higher." The boy's sense of security and acceptance shined right through his mask of embarrassment.

You don't have to carry pompoms or a megaphone to be a cheerleader. One of my close friends had an alcoholic father who left home early in Keith's life. But Keith had a star for a mom, and he's turned out to be one of the finest Christian men I know.

A talented athlete, Keith recently told me about the greatest event in his sports career. It was Dad's Night at his high school, in his senior year. All the fathers were lined up on the sidelines with their son's number fastened to their shirts. Keith felt alone and depressed as the special observance got underway.

Then suddenly he noticed someone standing in the line wearing his number. His heart skipped a beat: *Has Dad come home?* Looking closer, a tear entered his eye. There stood his mom, stately as any dad in the line, her hair tucked under her work hat, jeans pressed neatly, and number 24 displayed proudly on the back of her shirt.

CHEERLEADING IS FOR EVERYONE in the family—which is good, because it's highly contagious.

Any parent who's had to travel for a living knows the excitement and anticipation you feel that last day on the road, when you press through the night on a late flight or late drive to see your much-missed loved ones. After one long, winter road trip I came home at 2 A.M. to a house covered with "Welcome Home, Daddy!" posters, banners, cards, pictures, and poems. With a lump in my throat, I tiptoed through the confetti and back to my room, I opened my closet to find no less than thirty more signs. All four little ones had gotten into the homecoming preparation. The handwriting (some legible, some only scribbles)

spelled out "We missed you!" "We love you!"
"We're glad you're back!"

My eyes noticed especially a simple message
in runny watercolors. It said in my daughter's
simple eight-year-old honesty, "This is a very good
home."

In our very good home we have (as every
home has) our struggles, our tears, our unkind
words. But we are each other's biggest fans all
through the day and night. We believe in each
other, and verbalize that enthusiasm every chance
we get.

☞

—13—

A Coach

A boy is the only thing God can use to make a man.
— Cal Farley

AFTER WINNING the national collegiate basketball championship a few years ago, the smiling coach was given the ABC microphone with the question, "Aren't you proud of yourself now? Isn't this great for your career?"

"Nah, that's not what makes it great." The coach reached back into the crowd pressing around him to bring before the camera one of his jubilant players. "*This* is what it's all about," he said.

Great coaches don't work for titles and trophies. Their aim is to develop their players. Legendary football coach Bear Bryant expressed this philosophy in working with his players: "When something goes bad, *I* did it. When something goes not so good, *we* did it. When something goes great, *they* did it."

I played under several coaches in eleven years of football. Though some won more games than others, each season came and went just the same, and coach got the basic job done. But their coaching styles were definitely an assortment.

I still bristle at the memory of one man whose motivational method was to kick his players fiercely in the rear after they helplessly bent down into their stance for the next play. That was torture.

The two best coaches I had the opportunity of playing for were Ray Utley and Hayden Fry. Polar opposites in personality, both had unique styles that still help me set my sights as a dad.

Both men knew their players— not their weight, their speed, or their latest bench press, but their *hearts.* They knew that all players aren't motivated the same way. Some of us needed extra wind sprints. Some needed time after practice to talk. Others needed a raised voice or a half game on the bench. Our team was small and undertalented, but we went to the games united and motivated because those two men cared.

By knowing each player's individual bent, and by investing energy to bring out the best in that player, the great coach finds significance.

coach \kōch\ *n.* 1. Not a referee or an umpire, but a *teacher* who brings out the best in another. 2. If you love me, you know me; if you know me, you can show me.

Great fathers do it the same way.

One such father I know in Texas had a struggling seventeen-year-old son. He let him design and build his own house, a project that took two years to complete. With his father as "coach," the boy laid every log, drove every nail, poured every footing, and tacked on every shingle. When the fantastic experience was over, so were the teenage years . . . and *two friends* walked away, proudly.

Another dad found his father-son nitch in race cars. The two of them bought twin cars and traveled the nation racing together. In one recent race, the son took the cup after unintentionally forcing out his dad. But the dad walked away the bigger champion.

In the process of building a business empire, another father felt he was losing his son. After we talked, he decided to take off his business suit at night and put on mechanic's clothes to help his son work on his Volkswagen. He's finding his son again.

My own dad towed a Model A Ford six hundred miles so my brother could have a success experience rebuilding that antique under Daddy's guidance.

COACHES SELDOM GO OUT on the playing field during game time. For a father too, there comes a time to stay on the sidelines while his child goes alone into the arena to face the game of life. Our influence now depends solely on the job we did before the game— teaching, training, encouraging, preparing our son or daughter for this moment.

That takes faith.

It happens every time my daughter goes on a date or my son catches the bus to go to school. They go without their cheerleader-mom and without their father-coach.

It keeps us on our knees— a good place for a cheerleader and coach to be.

The key to winning these games is practicing hard and praying heartily. My daddy always reminded me to work like it all depends on me, and pray like it all depends on God. "Between the two of you," he said, "you'll come out a winner."

THE PRACTICE FIELD is yours and mine— the place to stay close to our children, to direct and nurture them. Good practice makes good games.

But the playing field belongs to our kids and God. It's the time for trust. It's the time for growth, the growth that is a mystery known only to God. To Him we pray. To Him goes the glory for the victories we'll see.

☞

GREAT COACHES

Bear Bryant—
"HE CARED FOR HIS PLAYERS"

by Gene Stallings

It was midnight. On the following day we were to play Baylor University. Texas A&M was in the midst of Bear Bryant's worst season (1 win, 9 losses) in his thirty-eight years of coaching. He came into the football dormitory and called the entire team into the lobby. He opened his Bible, and in his customary down-to-earth manner retold the parable of the mustard seed.

I'll never forget the concern for us, as people, that he communicated that night. He felt the hurt and embarrassment we and our families were feeling. He told us we didn't have much in the eyes of the public, but that we were winners if we didn't give up. He helped us believe we'd win in a bigger game—the Game of Life.

Three years later, we won the Southwest Conference Championship and for a while were number one in the nation.

Bear Bryant, who went on to become the winningest coach in football history, was unsurpassed in his profession because he cared for his players. Only those of us who had the privilege of playing for "The Bear" really know how much he cared. He was tough and intense, but he loved us from his heart. The love we felt from him translated into victory after victory, because love brings out the best in people.

Most coaches get the maximum out of some players, but Coach Bryant got the maximum out of all of them. You didn't want to disappoint this man who cared for you.

It didn't take a superstar to win his care. If you were Joe Namath you felt it, and if you barely made the team you felt it. He'd handle you gently when you made a bad play. He never criticized a player publicly. And if you had a special need, you could depend on Coach Bryant to help you out.

He always told us never to get too big or too busy to go to church on Sunday or to take time to write our moms and dads. I loved him for the man he was, for what he stood for, and for what he did for people.

After playing under him and being on his coaching staff, I took the reins at Texas A&M, where he had been my coach a decade before. Ironically, we won the Southwest Conference championship and met my teacher and his Alabama team in the Cotton Bowl. On that unforgettable day, A&M beat Alabama. After the game, instead of customarily shaking my hand, Coach Bryant picked me up to carry me off the field. Later he came over to our locker room. I excused myself from reporters to meet him at the door. He said candidly, "I didn't come to see you; I came to congratulate your players. They outplayed mine, and I want to tell them how much I respect them for it."

Bear Bryant once told the sports world that he retired from coaching because he felt the players deserved better than he was giving them. No one agreed. There's never been any better.

John Wooden—
"NEVER DEPARTING FROM THE FUNDAMENTALS"

by Ralph Drollinger

I had just arrived as a freshman at UCLA to play under John Wooden, the most successful college basketball coach in history. We were fifteen former high school All-Americans, later to become the season's national champions.

And here we were on the first day of practice . . . learning how to properly put on our socks and shoes. *Didn't I learn this in first grade?* I thought.

Lesson one was with the socks. Under his close scrutiny, Coach Wooden had us carefully roll them up, like you would your shirt-sleeves. Next we laboriously unrolled them up and over our feet toward the calf muscle. Like Sherlock Holmes with a magnifying glass, he paced the room during the process looking for a tiny, sinful wrinkle in the rows of thirty oversized white feet. He had us run our hands several times over the cotton surface to make sure we'd executed the fundamentals correctly.

The next lesson was on lacing up your shoes. "You mustn't pull the top laces until you put tension in the bottom laces," he said with obvious years of experience. I didn't question his sanity. Echoes of success permeated the place, casting me in a spell of reverential belief that this was the right thing to be doing the first day of practice.

After graduating from UCLA, having performed the same fundamental procedure for years in professional competition, I found myself still executing it carefully. My uneducated teammates smarted at me as I patiently applied my footwear, but that didn't bug me. I knew from experience that more smarting would soon occur after practice— on their feet.

Coach Wooden's philosophy stressed the proper execution of the fundamentals, which were learned by daily repetition. His approach to a seemingly complex game was simple and basic, never departing from the fundamentals.

Since you couldn't perform these basic maneuvers with blistered feet, the wise coach began his sessions lecturing on socks and shoes. After dressing our feet, we would do drills without the ball so our concentration centered on executing the physical motion correctly rather than on the results. This helped form good habits, which are difficult to learn if you're temporarily having good results with poor habits.

We who desire to be excellent Christian parents and leaders can learn a main ingredient of success from one of sport history's greatest coaches— a man who so vividly exemplified the scriptural principle of repeating continually the grass-roots basics. Day after day, we must properly put on our socks and shoes . . . to "run the race so as to win the prize."

Tom Landry—
"CREATIVE GENIUS"

by Walt Garrison

When I came to Dallas in 1966 we were far from being the NFL's best team. We all were firmly convinced that very soon we would be. We were playing for the best coach in the game . . . the creative genius of the National Football League.

A creative coach lets you know where you're going and the steps it will take to get there. I learned how the game all fit together from Tom Landry. He taught us how to combine discipline, knowledge, conditioning, motivation, goal-setting, confidence, and control to build a winning team.

He believed we had the information to beat anyone. So I studied harder at Dallas than I ever did in college. He taught us that if we were better prepared, we'd win. Football is a game of the split-second edge, and the team that has it will beat its opponent. With our trips, divides, motions, sings, and preshifts we could confuse the defense for a fraction of a second and get that edge. We began to win. Soon we were in the Super Bowl.

He has a creative way of handling people too. When you got stomped, he'd find something good you did to comment on and build you up. When you did great and felt pretty confident, he'd bring you down to earth.

Against Philadelphia one Sunday I pulled in an easy pass with one hand. During the film session on Monday everyone laughed and made remarks like "Way to make it look easy." When they quieted down I heard Coach Landry say softly, "Don't ever drop one." I got the message.

During the first half of the 1970 Super Bowl I got beat up all over. I was broken and bruised worse than I had ever been. On the bench the trainer was working with my injuries. Coach Landry walked by and spoke to the trainer: "Can he play?"

"I don't know," was the reply.

"I hope so," Landry said. "We need him."

I was back after halftime, and caught a touchdown pass to help us win. I would have played if my leg was cut off. Just to hear him say that word of encouragement was like a trumpet blast.

When you have faith in a man, you'll run through brick walls for him.

The things Coach Landry taught me mean more to me today than they did when I played for him. I've found that the same things that win on the football field also bring victory in the family and in life as well.

— 14 —

Strengths & Weaknesses

I HAD A SERIOUS PROBLEM during my wife's second pregnancy. My first little girl (who turned out to be virtually a clone of her mom) had so won my heart that I didn't think I could ever love another child as I did her.

The birth of number two easily remedied the problem!

I found it easy to love both girls equally. But I also learned that it takes a whole different part of me to love each one. The only thing they seem to have in common is a last name.

In fact, I even seriously questioned whether second daughter Courtney had the same parents as number one Jamie. Genetics sure deals some interesting hands! Jamie the brunette is reserved, thoughtful, consistent, even-tempered. Courtney the blonde is outgoing, straightforward, spontaneous, excitable.

The two boys who followed them continued the neat trick of pulling totally unique personalities from the same set of parental genes. Our third child Brady is sensitive, esthetic, self-disciplined, conscientious, analytical. Cooper, fourth in line, is friendly, talkative, enthusiastic, carefree, generous.

Everytime I go into a different kid's room, I have to change hats.

If I disciplined Cooper the same way I disciplined Jamie, he'd think he was a total failure and might never recover. One good stern look can take care of Cooper for a month.

Jamie cries over an injured goldfish but never shed a tear during a spanking. Courtney cries at the first mention of discipline, but might just as quickly push a dog aside as pet him.

Courtney writes great "I'm sorry" notes after she's been corrected. Jamie keeps her cool.

I'm thoroughly enjoying the process of studying and understanding the strengths and weaknesses of our kids . . . and seeing how uniquely and wonderfully each one has been gifted. It's an adventure every parent can have.

BUT FIRST, here's a list of What Not to Do as you go along:

1. Never compare a daughter's weakness to her mother's strength.

2. Never compare a son's weakness to his father's strength.

3. Never compare one sibling's weakness to another's strength.

4. Don't insist on or expect the same response from any two children in the same situation.

5. Never focus on the negative side of a child's personality.

6. Never fail to notice the evidence of a child's strengths; instead, take every opportunity to build them up even more.

Finally . . . and most importantly:

7. Never stop learning more. Aim continually to *really* know your child.

OUR CHILDREN'S PERSONALITIES are wonderfully created— uniquely programmed by God. One result is that each child's shortcomings cause him to need and depend on his siblings and parents in order to reach his full potential. It's a process of mutual enabling and strengthening . . . and it's good!

Another result is that each child's list of strengths has a corresponding set of weaknesses. And that's good too.

Why?

The fine art of successful parenting involves focusing on and building up the strengths of each child, and thereby overcoming the weaknesses. But if you're like me (and like ninety-nine percent of all parents), your tendency much of the time will be to focus on the weaknesses. If we do, the result in the child's life may well be low self-esteem, a sense of acceptance based only on performance, moodiness and depression, susceptibility to peer pressure, and a greater likelihood of drug and alcohol use and premarital sex.

Rather than focusing on a child's evident weaknesses, which we tend to see clearly, you can instead use these as clues to understand that child's strengths.

My good friend Wes Neal has studied in depth this area of strengths and corresponding weaknesses, and in the chart on the next page I pass along his observations to stimulate your thoughts in this area.

The first step, when a weakness in your child surfaces, is to look for the strength that's like a siamese twin of that weakness. Discipline yourself not to focus on the weakness, but to instead search for the strength— like a gold nugget in a pile of ore. Do this consistently and you'll be well on your way to helping that child perfect and refine the treasure in his personality.

SOME CHARACTER STRENGTHS . . .
AND THEIR RELATED WEAKNESSES

Analytical	Critical
Appreciative	Insincere
Assertive	Domineering
Communicative	Overtalkative
Concerned	Worrying
Confident	Self-sufficient
Counseling	"Know-it-all"
Courageous	Reckless
Curious	Nosey
Determined	Stubborn
Diplomatic, Tactful	Weak-willed
Effective	Rigid
Encouraging	Flattering
Expressive	Flowery
Forgiving	Overlenient
Generous	Wasteful
Imaginative	Day-dreaming
Listening	Noncommunicative
Loyal	Idolizing
Moral	Judgmental
Obedient	Overdependent
Open-minded	Indecisive
Optimistic	Unrealistic
Orderly	Perfectionistic
Sensitive	Oversensitive
Spontaneous	Undisciplined
Stable	Dull
Straightforward	Harsh
Thrifty	Stingy
Tolerant	Fainthearted

Do your kids a favor today: Complete the chart on the next page (or use a sheet of paper with three columns marked off). In the first two columns, under the headings "Strengths" and "Weaknesses," make a list of each child's evident character qualities, both positive and negative. Put corresponding strengths and weaknesses on the same line. Remember, your *focus* is to be on each child's positive qualities. If his weaknesses come to mind more readily, use these simply as clues to uncover the matching strengths.

In the third column, under the heading "My Goals," list ideas on how you can *constructively* build up each strength . . . and overcome the corresponding weakness without damaging the child's self-image.

☞

STRENGTH	CORRESPONDING WEAKNESS	MY GOALS

—15—

50 Phrases to Encourage Your Child

(For Everyday Use)

1. You're so much fun to be around!

2. You get better at that every time I see you. Way to go!

3. Hang on a second while I call *Sports Illustrated*—they'll want a picture of this!

4. I'm going to brag about this. That's great!

5. I look up to you!

6.   That's the best _____ I've ever seen!

7.   You are *so* thoughtful!

8.   This is a tremendous improvement!

9.   Good for you!

10. You're such a joy to us!

11. I never did that well when I was your age!

12. Can I put this on the bulletin board at the office so I can see it every day?

13. You handled that beautifully!

14. That's incredible!

15. You're always teaching me something wonderful!

16. They just didn't make kids as good as you when I was growing up!

17. You're really special to me— and getting more special every day!

18. Keep that up and you'll be the world champion someday!

19. I really enjoy being with you!

20. What a super effort!

---

grace /grās/ *n.* 1. Love and protection freely bestowed. 2. No strings attached. 3. Christmas and your birthday, every day of the year.

21. The guy who marries you will be so lucky!

22. That's worth a trophy ten feet high!

23. Your mom and I are so grateful to be your parents!

24. I need to get word to the White House about this— the President will want to know about it!

25. I really enjoy your smile!

26. That's fabulous!

27. There you go! That's it!

28. You're so helpful! Thank you!

29. You're going to make it!

30. God is truly a miracle worker— to produce a kid as great as you from ordinary parents like us!

31. I wish I could have done it that well!

32. You'll always be in my hall of fame!

33. I'm *impressed!*

34. I know you worked very hard on that. Wonderful job!

35. You're the best!

36. You sure know how to do it right! Outstanding!

37. I love to hear your laugh!

38. You're something else!

39.   That's amazing! How did you do that?

40.   You take my breath away!

41.   You never cease to amaze me!

42.   I really like that!

43.   Sensational!

44.   Absolutely superb!

45.   I believe in you!

46.   Excellent! That's the way to do it!

48.   Fantastic!

49.   You make me *so* happy!

50.   I love you!

PART IV

Safe at Home

What you value, your child will value.

—16—

Oh, Those X-ray Eyes!

Dear Miss Ellerby:
When I grow up, I want to do exactly
what you do. Please do it better.
— Letter from a child to television
news commentator Linda Ellerby

YOUR GREATEST OPPORTUNITY, bar none, to teach your kids the character qualities you want to see in their lives is the way you live your daily life. They watch every move you make, hear every tone of your voice, and seem to be especially keen at picking up actions and attitudes that contradict your verbal messages.

I believe this is the most sensitive area of effective leadership in the home. It's also the kind of parenting that carries the highest price tag. It will probably cost you a lot in terms of giving up pride, relinquishing certain habits, shaping up many neglected areas of your personal life, and learning how to change and adapt.

There is so much at stake in a child's tender years. How can we gamble with that child's perceptions and values by maintaining areas of questionable behavior in our lifestyle?

Children do give their parents room for failure— but in general they cling to what they see in their parents everyday lives. The parent who tries to hide certain personal habits from his child— or who tries to rationalize actions that are even remotely inconsistent with the lifestyle he wants his child to live by— is tiptoeing on thin ice, and at the very least will cause inconsistencies in his child's behavior.

Our kids have x-ray eyes when it comes to seeing our inconsistencies. *Congruence*, that old mathematical term from plane geometry class, comes back to haunt me. Every day I need to examine my habits to see if they match what I really want to see in my kids' lives. My lifestyle at home must set the pace for how I want my children to live.

More than anything else I want them to see a daddy whose number one goal in life is to love God with all his heart. I want them to see in me the ability to ask for forgiveness and to get back up

ex·am·ple \ĭg-zăm-pĕl\ *n.* 1. The kind of life that keeps prompting the comment, "When I grow up, I want to be like you"; a model worthy of imitation. 2. "Do as I do."

after I've fallen on my face in failure (which I seem to do regularly). I want them to see that integrity is more important than making a dime or a dollar. I want them to see me treating my body with purity, diligently training it for the awesome responsibility of being a temple of the Holy Spirit.

Finally, I want them to see how their very average Dad loves their very priceless Mommy with uncompromising dedication . . . and would walk around this planet to convince his children how precious each one of them is as well.

NO PRICE TAG

A successful parent's example can't be bought . . . at any price.

The story is told of a desperate businessman who propositioned his receptionist with an offer for an extramarital affair. When rebuffed, he added $1,000 to make the offer more attractive— knowing that she and her husband were undergoing financial difficulty. Reluctantly, she accepted.

Then he lowered his bid to $100.

"A hundred dollars!" she exclaimed. "What kind of a woman do you think I am?"

"You've already shown me what *kind* of woman you are," he returned. "Now I just want to know your price."

If there's a price tag on the principles I want to live by . . . the principles I want my children to

gain from our home . . . then eventually, someone will name it and I'll fall.

If I'm not willing to keep those principles so
priceless that I always *live out* those qualities . . .
then my teaching to my children is in vain.

Example is to training a child what railroad
tracks are to a freight train, or wings to an
airplane. Knowing that his child's eyes are always
watching, an effective parent will not sell out his
lifestyle at any price.

As I counsel America's hurting teenagers I so
often find that their bad habits and major failures
were learned from the example of their mom and
dad. The carpet into my office has a worn
pathway of teenagers who tell the same tragic
story. . . .

*Sixteen-year-old, brown-eyed Mary had an
abortion.*
> Her mom has a boyfriend.

*Eighteen-year-old Andy went to jail with two
DWI's.*
> His daddy caps every evening with
> martinis.

Martin has a hard time telling the truth.
> His dad evades the IRS with falsified
> financial reports.

Sally is a strong-willed, rebellious sixteen-year-old.
> Sally's mom is the family dictator.

Bill lost his driver's licence over speeding tickets.
> Bill's parents use fuzz-busters in their
> cars.

Amy and Greg wage a constant sibling rivalry.
>Their dad is snappy and quick-
>tempered with both of them.

*Julie is the most unpopular kid at school because
she hits anyone who gets in her way.*
>Her body bears the marks of hasty
>backhands from her demanding
>mother.

It would be naive to say every problem a
teenager experiences is a direct result of an
inconsistency in a parent's life. Some of the finest
parents I know today are having great problems
with their teenagers.

But most child psychologists agree that
children often become aggravated, rebellious, and
irresponsible as they misunderstand and imitate
the behavior they see in their parents.

THE GREATEST DEBT

The greatest part of my extensive
indebtedness to my parents is for how I saw them
live their lives.

I've had time to forget my dad's faults and
mistakes during our growing up years, and I'm
sure he had his share. But I'm firmly convinced
that he made (and continues to make) many
sacrifices to be a man who walks his talk. I can't
tell you how much I respect him because of it!

Frankly, I can't tell you anything he ever told
me about loving a wife . . . but I'll never forget
seeing the love notes he often left my mom when

he left our house early for work.   Nor will I forget
the respect and tenderness he always showed her.

Daddy's knees must be calloused from his
consistent evening quiet time before the Lord. He
didn't need to talk with us about the importance
of prayer. He earned the right to demand purity of
speech in our lives because I never heard him
utter a four-letter word.

I don't remember Mom telling us how happy
we'd be as parents some day if we learned the joy
of serving our spouses and children . . . but I
cherish the memories of watching her gather and
wash our dirty clothes, scrub our dirty dishes,
and with a soft smile carefully pack our lunches
for school. The wrinkles on her precious face are
the trophies of the pleasure she learned to derive
as she served my daddy and her three often
ungrateful sons day after day after day.

Oscar Daddy

Every spring I encourage my wife to go on a
week's vacation with her girlfriends. With four
children, a husband, a demanding job, and a
house to keep, she needs it! My number-one
priority in setting an example as a father is to
show my appreciation and admiration for the one
in our home who serves as psychologist,
sociologist, director of purchasing, financial
planner, household executive, referee, maitre d',
sanitation supervisor, counselor-in-chief, and
expert in pediatrics, community relations, religion,
economics, entertainment and horticulture— my
wife! Another reason for having her leave for a

while is so I can understand and appreciate even better all that she does each day.

One such spring, after "batching it" for six days, I awoke with lingering tiredness on a beautiful Easter morning. For this special day I had been left with a new roll of film and brand-new hand-sewn Easter clothes for our growing foursome.

Being a clutz around the house, it was all I could do to get all four little bodies bathed and dried . . . while getting breakfast cooked, Sesame Street placemats laid (featuring separately Burt, Ernie, Big Bird, the Cookie Monster, and Oscar the Grouch), and the table set . . . then getting Easter clothes secured right-side-out for Mommie's welcome-home picture. My nerves were frazzled.

The straw that broke the camel's back was the white tights that somehow had to go over the plump little legs and bottoms of my two daughters. They might have fit their Barbie dolls, but certainly the manufacturer didn't have a fumble-fingered bachelor in mind when the nylon

There are little eyes upon you
and they're watching night and day;
there are little ears that quickly
take in every word you say;
there are little hands all eager
to do anything you do;
and little fellows dreaming
of the day they'll be like you . . .

was measured for this unreasonable task of dressing up two growing girls. I tried and tried to make them stretch to their wastes. Wrinkled ankles and baggy crotch was the best I could do.

Finally, we sat down to the lukewarm oatmeal amid accusations that "paste" was a better description of my concoction. While reaching out to join hands in prayer, I knocked a placemat on the floor. It happened to be Oscar the Grouch. I went on with the prayer, saying hurriedly, "Dear Lord, thank you for Easter and the joy of this day. And thank you for the food. Amen."

Leaning down to pick up the placemat, a small voice whispered in the air, "You better have Oscar today, Dad."

"What did you say?" I snapped at our oldest, whose smirk gave away the source.

"I just thought you might want to keep the Oscar placemat today," she said.

I heard her correctly the first time. "What did you mean by that remark?" I demanded.

She cleared her throat courageously. "Well, you prayed about the joy of Easter but it's sort of hard to believe, because you're kind of a grouch this morning."

> . . . You are setting an example
> every day in all you do
> for the little fellows wanting
> to grow up and be like you.

We all got tickled, and laughed together at Oscar Daddy. But she was right, and the truth penetrated through the humor. I made a fresh determination to work— and I mean *work*— on setting a better example. Boy, do I fail! And usually the letdowns don't end with laughter as at my Oscar Easter breakfast. But the results have been well worth the sweat.

☞

—17—

That's Not In There, God!

I WAS IN A CAFE in Nashville, calling home to Southern Missouri after two weeks of lonesome business travel. Debbie Jo told me she had just come from her prized traditional evening time of tucking the children into bed with prayers. As she had said good night to our two boys in their Super Hero pajamas, Super Cooper said he wanted to memorize a new Bible verse so he could tell it to his Daddy when he came home. "Get out my Bible," he said in his four-year-old dialect, "and wead me one, okay?"

"Cooper," she replied, "the lights are out— can I just *tell* you one?"

191

"Okay."

She pulled out the old standby. "A good verse for every child to know is: 'Children, obey your parents, for this is pleasing to God.' "

There was a long pause. Finally Cooper spoke. "That's not in there, Mommy."

"Yes it is, Sweetheart."

"No," he protested, "I think you just made that one up."

I roared with laughter as Debbie Jo gave the account over the telephone. After I hung up and walked back to my table, the truth struck my heart like a sword. That's *exactly* what I tell God when I keep a safe distance from a Bible verse that demands not only my attention but my action— especially when He asks me to change something I don't want to change.

That's not in there, God!

Oh, yes it is! All of it is in there, and it's all from our infinitely wise parent in heaven who cared enough to communicate His truths in a love letter written literally with His blood.

The passage that today presses me onward into action, sacrifice, planning, and time management is Deuteronomy 6:5-9.

> And you shall love the Lord your God with all your heart and with all your soul and with all your might. And these words, which I am commanding you today, shall be on your heart; and you shall teach them diligently to your sons and shall talk of

them when you sit in your house and when you
walk by the way and when you lie down and when
you rise up. And you shall bind them as a sign on
your hand and they shall be as frontals on your
forehead. And you shall write them on the
doorposts of your house and on your gates.

If I could place in your palm a 393-page book
that would absolutely guarantee you a successful
multimillion-dollar business, would you read it?
Would you memorize key statements in it? Would
you think about it continually as you went about
your business day by day and week by week?
Undoubtedly you would.

I can't promise you that kind of business
experience, but God's book promises you many
times more than a multimillion-dollar value. It
promises you a successful future for your children
if you teach them His Word day after day, if you
memorize it together night after night, and apply it
in your home in every situation. Yet of all the kids
I've surveyed on this, only eight percent have
parents who take God at His Word and memorize
Scripture together consistently as a family.

AN INSIDE LOOK

A friend of mine named Jack Herschend built
from scratch one of the country's most creative
theme parks and named it Silver Dollar City. It
began humbly enough with a small general store
atop a large, beautiful crystal cave here in
Southern Missouri. In the thirty years since

then, Jack has put every available penny into his
dream of expanding the enterprise into a park that
would literally bring back to life the Ozarks of the
1880s.

Today Silver Dollar City is a multimillion-
dollar mix of clever attractions, rides, and craft
displays, all in a hillbilly atmosphere. But the
feature that gets by far the highest rate of
attention for the money it cost to create is a silver-
dollar sized hole in an out-of-the-way fence. The
hole is just about eye-level to a twelve-year-old
boy.   A small sign above the hole reads, "Don't
Look In This Hole." Needless to say, no one
passes by without a peek. Behind the hole is a
ridiculous picture that makes you wonder why
you bothered looking.

In the midst of all the media messages that
constantly contend for your family's attention, I'd
like to erect a simple fence with a peephole at your
eye level, with a "Don't Look" sign on top to work
the same magic it does on the fence in Silver
Dollar City.

Step up to the old weathered wood, wink
your left eye, and put your right squarely in the
middle of the peephole. What you'll see could be
the most compelling picture your parenting eyes
will ever behold.

You recognize immediately the prominent
figure in the foreground: He is tall, lean, dark,
bearded . . . his thin, granite face highlighted by
heavy eyebrows set above eyes that are deep and
penetrating, seemingly with power both to stare
into your heart and to grace it with compassion.

With a voice as powerful as his gaze, Lincoln now speaks. His words, well over a century old, are like the brush strokes of a skilled master, painting an alarming portrait of prophetic wisdom for today:

> We have grown in numbers, wealth and power as no other nation has grown, but we have forgotten God. We have forgotten the gracious hand that preserved us in peace and multiplied and enriched and strengthened us. We have vainly imagined that all of these blessings were produced by some superior virtue and wisdom of our own. . . . Intoxicated with unbroken success, we have become too self-sufficient to feel the necessity of redeeming and preserving grace, too proud to pray to the God that made us.

The painter's brush is passed from Honest Abe to the the even greater hands of the God whom Lincoln worshiped, and these words are added to the masterpiece, echoing from the First Psalm:

> *How blessed is the man (every father and mother,*
> *   every boy and girl) . . .*
> *whose delight is in the law of the Lord,*
> *   and on His law he meditates day and night.*
> *He will be like a tree firmly planted by*
> *   streams of water,*
> *   which yields its fruit in its season*
> *and its leaf does not wither.*
> *   In whatever he does, he prospers.*

Press your eye even closer and look intently: In the background, a choir of saintly fathers and mothers from ages past completes the picture. As you scan first one face and then another and another, each figure speaks with earnest, pleading counsel: "The greatest thing you can do for your children is to pitch a tent in their minds where the treasure chest of God's Word can dwell."

WHEN YOU'RE SURE the entire scene is fixed firmly in mind, turn around to examine your own home. Does the heartbeat of Scripture sound in every life?

Our kids need to memorize the First Psalm and learn how essential it is not to walk in the counsel of the wicked, but instead to meditate on

OUR LITTLE COOPER was five years old, and well on his way to memorizing his third chapter in the Bible. We were memorizing together Matthew chapter five, from the Sermon on the Mount. One night just before bedtime we were looking at verse eighteen, where God commands all His children to "Let your light so shine . . ."

"Cooper," I exclaimed, "that's exactly the kind of boy you are; you let your light shine better than anyone I know!"

His face beamed with excitement and confidence. "I know, Dad. It's because I sleep at night with my Bible underneath my pillow."

God's Word day and night. Their computers must be programmed with the cleansing power of the knowledge of God's will in their lives.

As parents we must teach them Psalm 23, whose words will convey to their hearts the security and peace of knowing the Lord as their Shepherd.

They need to learn Philippians 2, and then together experience the deepened joy of a family that practices the Christlike unselfishness of loving each other sacrificially.

Together with our children we must memorize Matthew 5, and become completely convinced that true happiness depends on trusting Christ.

From memorizing portions of John's gospel we and our children must see the divine characteristics of Jesus, and give back to Him our praise and worship.

THE MAGIC

I'LL NEVER FORGET the moment when my inadequacy for the task of fatherhood first dawned on me. Our firstborn daughter was sleeping tenderly in her crib at age six months. As I watched her, I was suddenly overcome with a sense of responsibility, love, and humility. "God!" I prayed, "I can't handle this alone. No way can I be this little doll's ultimate authority. I need you to take over the job."

Slowly— but consistently— I began to

memorize Scripture, Once her third birthday had
passed, I began passing on to her what I had
memorized, verse by verse. She's now caught up
with me, because her brain works at 78 RPM and
mine still plays at 33⅓.

As we continue memorizing, the magic comes
especially in two different ways.

First, by reinforcing the fact the God and His
word are her authorities in life, it gives her
"temporary daddy" the freedom to fail and a basis
for recognizing and being forgiven for that failure.
An early example came when she was still three,
and I swatted her on the bottom in a moment of
anger. I knew it was wrong when my hand stung
the seat of her pants and her look of betrayal
caught my eye. She already was old enough to
perceive the difference between a deserved
spanking and this angered blow that was more a
release of my frustration than an effort to
discipline in love. That night as we prayed
together I asked for the forgiveness of God and the
forgiveness of that three-year-old. I promised her
that though I knew my need to discipline her
when she deserved it, by God's grace I would
never hit her again in anger.

If she had no higher authority in life than
me, she would be crushed to despair by my
shortcomings, and I would tend to wear some false
mask of ego to try to hide the fact that her hero
was imperfect. Fortunately, she now understands
that God, her truly highest authority, is in every
way perfect, and is my Lord and Savior just as He
is hers. In that shared understanding we can
pursue those precious moments of reconciliation

whenever we need to.

The second payoff of Scripture memory at home is apparent when dealing with crises. If one of the kids is selfishly hoarding a toy, I can skip the lecture and instead say, "Brady, what's the verse from Philippians we learned last night?"

"Have this attitude in yourselves which is also in Christ Jesus."

"Great job, Buddy. What kind of attitude did Jesus have, anyway?"

"A good one," he answers soberly.

"Was it selfish or unselfish?"

"Unselfish."

"Okay, what kind of attitude are you wrestling with right now?"

"Selfish." (He said it. I didn't have to.)

"Is that what you want to have today?"

"No, sir."

"What would Jesus do, Brady?"

"Change His attitude and give Cooper the toy."

"Will you do that?"

"Yes, sir."

It has worked for us time after time after time. It's amazing how God's Word fits every situation. Just as He promises, "My word . . .

will not return to me void."

God's Word is eternal. It transcends time, and that means it also fits with custom-tailored accuracy the life of each child, regardless of the age. From preschool to high school graduation and beyond, God's word always contains the building blocks for true maturity.

IF IT'S DONE a little every day, I find it easy to help even small children memorize Scripture. In our family we began with each child at age three, and we plan to persistently practice it with them until they go off to college.

AS THE TEEN YEARS approached in our home, we began another daily pattern in our lifestyle that has really been a Grand Slam. (If I could start over again, I would begin it much sooner.) First thing in the morning we all pile into one bed and have a short family devotional, focusing on applying the principles from the verse we memorized the night before. The most interesting "family devos" are the ones led by one of the kids after a fifteen-minute shared planning time with me the day before.

Honestly, it's the very best thing in our day!

FOR TEENS TOO

Whenever I take a trip with a group of teenagers, we plan not only a lot of crazy, fun

experiences, but also a Scripture memory
project— a short chapter that we learn along the
way, reviewing it each time we make a stop. When
the trip is complete, we return home with much
more than exciting memories and empty pockets—
we've also invested into our hearts a portion of
God's eternal, protective Word.

☞

—18—

Discipline Is a Lifestyle

"The rod of reproof gives wisdom and joy"—
inspired are these words from above.
So parents take heed,
for your child is in need
of this balance of firmness and love.

IF YOU SCREAM one more time, I'll give you a tranquilizer," the young mother threatened.

Even the takeoff roar of the 747 jet engines couldn't muffle the piercing, continuous screams of her three-year-old daughter in the seat just behind mine. Everyone on board was wishing these two had stayed home.

The child was begging for discipline. She knew instinctively that her bottom needed firm attention. But her mother didn't have the loving courage to give it . . . or perhaps she was

203

addicted to yet another new and illusory theory of
child development. Her ultramodern remedy for
the undisciplined child was medication. In twelve
or fifteen years, another drug addict will roam the
streets looking for an instant fix.

"Discipline me!" "Give me rules!" "Punish
me when I break them!" By our very nature we
cry out for discipline, and the Bible commands us
to lovingly discipline our children. Discipline
minus love equals rebellion, but love minus
discipline equals insecurity.

We are a nation of extremes. Our tea must
be either piping hot or Arctic-ice cold. Our
famous football players are giants, and our
heralded gymnasts are tiny tots. We don't simply
eat right—we crash diet. We don't just jog—we
run marathons. So it is with our disciplinary
tactics. Many children I counsel are so beat down
physically or emotionally they can't see straight.
They think their middle name is Shut Up and
their back side is their father's belt rack.

For girls from this background, the first guy
who comes along and says "I love you" will usually
find a gullible sex object. For the boys, if they
can't get rid of their aggression on the football
field, a six-pack of beer and a Saturday night
street fight will almost always be enticing. Both

dis·ci·pline \dĭs-ĭ-plĭn\ *n.* 1. Security in
action. 2. "This hurts me more than it hurts
you." 3. Payment for a misdeed, "called" in
fairness. 4. Because love cares enough to
rend the very best.

sexes are easy prey for drug pushers, and neither has a fraction of a chance to maintain a happy marriage of their own.

Flip the coin and meet the Sugar Lump kids. Their mothers are really their attorneys, rushing quickly to their defense if anyone (including their passive fathers) tries to correct or scold these little princes and angels. The fathers are usually not around enough to see the impending problem or to know their child's true needs.

And so . . .

At an early age these kids squeal and grunt and stomp when they're unhappy or don't get their way, and bang their trays when they're hungry. The girls at age six have the latest hairstyle and designer clothes, are wearing makeup a few years later, and by the time they enter junior high look as much like sixteen-year-old models as their genetics will allow.

For both boys and girls, any problems at school are always the teacher's fault. In their sports the coach is never right and the referee always needs new glasses.

Their early employment years are marked with failures and firings, and their marriages by selfishness and separation. When crises come in their lives, they fall apart, inside and out.

Protesting a midnight curfew, a seventeen-year-old in Los Angeles calls his mom a four-letter name and slams the door in a rage . . . leaving his dad speechless and withdrawn.

In Chicago, a fifteen-year-old dreams up new ways to hurt her mom in daily acts of rebellion, because her mom stands in the way of her relationship with a boyfriend who time after time has demonstrated deceitfulness and immaturity.

"You're too old-fashioned!" screams the Kansas City seventeen-year-old boy. "You never let me do anything, so I'm going on my own now." His single mother is tired of fighting. All she ever wanted for her son was his happiness . . . but he's ended up a spoiled, hot-headed misfit.

Andy reports to summer camp with deep bruises across his upper legs and an aggressive, unpredictable personality. Day after day he tests his counselor. He never adjusts to his cabin mates, and seems to believe that anything he wants badly enough he can get with his fists and elbows.

MARKS OF A LIFESTYLE

True discipline is a lifestyle. Making it happen depends on our following some basic rules. These ten guidelines are simple enough to write out—but living them out requires constant, relentless attention.

1. The sooner in the child's life you begin, the easier it is.

2. Mom and Dad can discuss their separate philosophies on discipline behind closed doors, but when they enter the arena, they should be of one mind—always supporting each other in discipline decisions.

3. If the rod is spared the child is spoiled, but if the rod is used in the wrong place or with the wrong motives or the wrong timing, the child will rebel at it every time.

4. Be careful about threats. If you warn a child to expect a certain kind of punishment, always follow through completely.

5. When a child breaks a rule, something corrective *always* needs to happen. For example: Lying always receives a spanking.

6. If respect is demanded in every conversation at home, heavy discipline will be required less frequently.

7. Every corrective action should be encircled by ten expressions of positive encouragement.

8. Spankings should always be both preceded and followed by expressions of love and support.

9. A child must be taught to cry softly, and never be allowed to scream in rebellion.

10. Never give up on a child.

These guidelines transcend personality differences and work with every kind of child— as we've learned in raising a stoic one, a jubilant one, a strong-willed one, and a compliant one.

LAYING THE FOUNDATION:
THE WORDS AND WAYS OF DISCIPLINE

The first word our children learned to say was *Please*. For the first few months it came out only as a "puh" sound, but even then nothing is given until that sound comes out. Squeals, grunts, and banging the plate get no rewards.

The second word they learned was "ta-ta" (one-year-old lingo for *thank you*). After it's been learned, if it isn't said, the reward is taken back.

It's amazing how easy it is to develop an attitude of gratefulness in a child with these simple ground rules. The child learns early that the world does not revolve around his needs and wants.

Understanding the meaning of a soft but firm *No* was also part of our children's early training. We left plants, antiques, and lamps where they looked best in the house, and as soon as the one-year-old reached for one of them he heard the No, and also had something else placed in his hands that was okay to play with or put in his mouth. The second time he reached for the forbidden item he received a similar warning. The third time, his hand was slapped. We then encouraged him and gave a hug to assure him he was loved.

Depending on the child's strength of will, that particular plant or lamp might be the battleground for several confrontations. But by being consistent and firm and loving, we ensured that the lesson was never forgotten.

Yes, Sir and *Yes, Ma'am* also were early

vocabulary. "Yeah" isn't acceptable. We believe respect for parental authority is something to be forged continuously. The good husband never lets the wife be spoken to disrespectfully, and vice versa. In a two-parent home, that respect is best learned by the child as the wife models it toward her husband. Likewise, the most effective way to teach sacrificial love is for the dad to love his wife "as Christ loved the church." The example of my mom and dad in this has been easy to follow, because they have always modeled a mutually submissive relationship.

More importantly, the reinforcing steel in the foundation of respect is a healthy fear of God and His commandments. A disciplinary system built on that foundation will require few spankings— but physical punishment will still on occasion be required.

My dad clearly laid down the basics in our family: "When you break a rule, you're going to be punished." He never hit us anywhere but on the bottom. He never left bruises . . . but he always left an impression.

The last whipping he gave me was one I'll never forget. I was a cocky junior high kid, and I got caught lying to my mom. It was a Friday night. All my daddy said was, "Bring me my belt on Sunday afternoon."

He said nothing more to me about it the rest of that evening or all day Saturday, but the discipline was taking its full effect. I lived that lie a hundred times before he met me on Sunday afternoon. The spanking was the easy part for me, because during the interim Daddy had accomplished two things. First, he allowed himself to calm down. I think he knew he would have hurt me if he spanked me in his anger immediately following my rebellious lie. Second, he let me discipline myself for a day and a half.

After the spanking, Mom was there to help

When I met Wesley at a monthly skating-rink youth rally, he was fourteen and had just been suspended from school for ten days.

Ten years later I was paying for his attorney to get him a second trial after he spent six long years in a state penitentiary for armed robbery. In the years between, Wes had been caught breaking the law eighteen times.

Wes's dad was an alcoholic and wasn't at home to discipline him. His mom didn't know how. And the juvenile officer just kept putting off his punishment.

When his time was finally paid and his young adulthood was behind him, he was released. He was convinced he was a new person. But he had been ingrained with the philosophy that not much really happens when you do something wrong. He had only been discplined once, so he continued smoking grass, drinking, and committing crimes.

One night he was caught with a firearm—shooting a warning shot in a fight—and authorities found a marijuana joint in his pocket. He called me (his only friend), and I went to see him. I found him lonely, frightened, clinging to the bars, and pleading for me to "put up the bond and get me out of this horrible place."

But I had made one of the toughest decisions I've ever had to make. "No, Wes, I'm not going to get you

Daddy reassure that even though I had broken one of the cardinal rules of the house, I was still dearly loved by them.

Daddy was good with a belt— and in the whole area of discipline— because he was fair and because he was firm. My first speeding ticket cost

out this time. You've repeatedly ripped people off since you've been out of prison, and now it's time to pay. I want you to be free, but I want more for you to build your character. You've got to grow up, Wes, and realize that when you do something wrong you must pay for it, all of it."

Not long afterward he called me from jail. While we talked of his upcoming trial, an operator came on the line with an emergency call. I quickly said goodbye to Wes, then took the call. It was a neighbor telling me he had just seen two boys stealing a new eight-horsepower gasoline motor from our lakefront. We used it for a boat pump. To them it would make a nice go-cart engine.

I jumped into a boat to pursue the suspects. After a chase, I caught them. By this time the father of one of the boys had allowed them to hide the stolen motor in his trailer. But the boys—scared of the police, scared of me, and scared of jail—confessed.

"Will you press charges?" they asked.

Having learned my lesson with Wes, I looked intently into the faces of those two confused teenagers and replied, "I'm not concerned about the pump, but I'm deeply concerned about you. Yes, I'm going to press charges and I hope they lock you up for a while." (I knew they wouldn't, but I wanted that impression to last as long as possible.)

me my driver's license for a month. Daddy made
it clear that the second would cause it to
disappear for six months, and the third one would
be bring a year of no driving, no matter what came
up during the penalty time. I knew that
evacuating town for a tornado wouldn't have been
enough reason for me to drive until the discipline
was complete. I didn't get that second ticket until
after I left home.

If I or one of my brothers got spanked at
school, then instead of criticizing the principal or
coach or finding fault with the system, Daddy
would spank us again when we got home.

He could discipline us for any kind of
drinking, smoking, cheating, or use of bad
language because *he* never did any of those. And
watching him stay under the speed limit while
driving over the years has helped make it seem
right to obey the law.

He wasn't perfect— and he was well aware of
his weaknesses— but he was totally sold out to
being an example to his kids. We were three hard-
headed boys with all the normal adolescent
energies, and each of us has made some very
stupid mistakes in our life, but the strong
foundation of discipline my parents built
relentlessly in our lives has always gotten us
through. They made it easy to come back to the
roots of serving, loving, and respecting one
another in the family.

⚷

—19—

My First Lady

She's totally woman, and totally mom,
and totally blessed with charm.

How do I love thee? Let me count the ways.
— Elizabeth Barrett Browning

IT WAS THE NIGHT BEFORE I would walk out
onto the gridiron on my first day of college
coaching.   I went into my bedroom, and there my
wife of fourteen months calmly informed me that
the flame in her heart for me had gone out, and
another had been lit for my best friend. The next
day, she moved home, and not long afterward my
best friend informed me of their wedding plans.

I cried every day for three months.

For some reason, forgiveness has never been
a problem— she is a terrific lady and he's a
wonderful man, and I never blamed either of them
for the departure. Yet the hurt planted a deep
scar on my heart that I'll die with.

Divorce is not only biblically wrong, but also

213

a devastating experience for the one who is left, as well as, eventually, for the one who leaves. And when children are involved— as my extensive teen counseling has proven to me repeatedly— they're especially broken by it, and their own hurts are seldom really considered or even understood.

But today I have a mysterious perspective about what that marriage failure meant in my own experience: I believe it was the greatest thing that ever happened to me. In the same way that God turned the pain, the rejection, and the ugly death of His Son into His most victorious moment in history . . . God also used my divorce to teach me how to love.

The only person alive who fully appreciates sight is someone blind who has undergone surgery and received his sight.

I was blind, and needed surgery . . . and God allowed it.

Losing a love taught me how to find one.

Later, when Debbie Jo said "I will," and then twelve months later said "I do," I was like the ugly toad who had just been kissed by the lovely princess. I'll never forget our seventh date when I first kissed her: I melted. Last night, I kissed her again for perhaps the ten-thousandth time. It was so much like the first, yet so much more wonderful.

Now there is no greater honor on earth for me than to walk into my home where a wife and four children truly love me, and I truly love them.

Romans 8:28 is indeed reality:

*And we know
that God causes all things
   to work together for good
to those who love God,
   to those who are called according
      to His purpose.*

We <u>know</u>.

<u>All</u> things.

For our *good*.

God is able— infinitely able— to make it happen, just as His word claims.

A dear old friend of mine suffered for years through the agonizingly slow decline and eventual death of his diseased wife. After a few years, he remarried. His new wife was healthy, and able to give him her love and affection. I remember watching her brush his gray hair as if he was her childhood dream come true.

Big, tender tears flowed from his eyes. No one had ever done that for him before.

I know how he feels. Oh, to be appreciated! Our hearts hunger for the taste of it.

Debbie Jo, my First Lady, does that for me. Whenever she wears a new wrinkle or a gray hair first appears . . . I count it as a sign of her ever-deepening love for me.

I remember hiding her engagement ring as the surprise in a box of Cracker Jacks, buried deep in the caramel corn and peanuts. I carefully resealed the box wrapper to keep it from looking tampered with. I pictured the look of surprise she would have.

We drove to the top of a three-hundred-foot cliff overlooking a vast Ozark lake . . . a Kodak perfect setting. The moment was rare. She opened the Cracker Jacks, and took a bite . . . then sputtered. It tasted like the odorous rubber cement I had used to reseal the package. She tossed the box over the cliff.

I caught it just as it left her hand. "Wait!" I screamed. "What about the surprise? *It* won't be stale!"

She squealed with excitement when my dear Grandmother's diamond caught her eye.

I was so much in love that day, though really I was just beginning to know what love was back

Debbie Jo loved the years of her life immediately following the birth of our four. She was a diaper changer par excellence. One child in a stroller, one in a backpack, and one preschooler at her side was routine for this champion. She also gave her love to her husband (and number-one fan), and as time permitted used her organizational and personnel skills to help keep my business and ministry progressing. Now she's able to do that even more.

There are times when she can work even more than a "full-time" work week—at other times she then. Nearly two decades later I feel I'm still discovering how to love her.

I don't recommend that anyone else try the same formula I did. But somehow God takes the broken pieces and puts them together in a new and more beautiful picture.

Why does it often take a tragedy to learn the lesson? Perhaps you will not wait to make the discovery until your children are gone from home, or you receive your first social security check. Perhaps it won't require a two-by-four across the skull to open your eyes, as it did for me.

A Success Story

Darrell and Norma were first-class newlyweds. With Federal Express speed Darrell

can put in only ten or twenty hours. But whatever the season of her life allows, she is committed to stay within trusted guidelines: Her career is her husband, her children, and her work, all three fitting under her priority of deep devotion to her heavenly Father, through an intimate relationship with His Son. Some days she fails. Some days she is frustrated with the effort required. But she is encouraged to persevere knowing that four kids still fight for the privilege to sit by her in the car . . . and her husband regularly scans his calendar to plan time alone with her.

would come home from his medical practice each
day to spend precious moments with his new
bride.

Soon daughter Tracy was born . . . then
came Michael, and finally Jason. The young mom
and dad "beat the Greek" as they defied all the
odds against raising polite, courteous, moral
children. Their enthusiasm for those three
trophies beat any I've ever observed in a family. A
twenty-by-twenty family room in their home is
literally wallpapered with a thousand or more
pictures that highlighted every experience of those
three children's growing-up years. I honestly get
more energy standing in that room than I did in
my first visit to the executive wing of the White
House.

But as the three children grew up, and their
parents spent their entire mental and emotional
resources on their kids, Darrell and Norma grew
apart from each other. They began to live like
strangers in the home. A cloud of bitterness
veiled the two hearts which once thrilled each
other in romance. A separation loomed in the
foreseeable future.

But many of us who knew them prayed . . .
and we prayed . . . and we prayed.

The countdown to their last child's high
school graduation grew ever closer to zero.
Divorce seemed inevitable.

Then God moved.

Darrell's medical practice took a jolt: Two
hard-to-replace employees had to leave, a long-

time partner also left, and he had to move his office to a new location. Just as he neared the autumn of his life, the season when he needed to begin slowing down, the pressure intensified.

He was drowning, reaching out for a rescue buoy. In desperation he turned to his wife . . . and Norma responded.

All the creative energies with which she had so successfully planned holidays and birthday parties and teen dances for her children now were channeled toward her husband's world. She filled the two vacated support jobs in his practice while also directing the completion of the new office— a six-month project. News of her expertise spread through the medical community, and literally hundreds of doctors and nurses came by the new office to behold the results of her talented resourcefulness.

Unaware of what was happening, I called Darrell and Norma's home for what I expected to be yet another counseling and consoling conversation about misery revealed. Norma answered and told me the story— and literally made me stand up in the airport phone booth with excitement. I asked her twice if I had dialed the wrong number.

Here was a brand new first lady full of love and an enriched self-image fostered by her husband.

"Do you know how to hug and kiss your new lover?" I asked.

"I'm a quick learner," she quickly replied.

The next time I flew into town I visited their house to behold this eighth wonder of the world. I spent the first half-hour with Darrell, who praised Norma and the God who made possible the renewal of his marriage. When Norma joined us, she spoke of Darrell as if he was her Prince Charming. Later I was given a tour of the new office, which Norma showed off in dignity and joy as the place where she loved to serve her husband.

☞

—20—

The Teenage Years...the Best Years

When a child turns thirteen you put him in a barrel
with only a hole to feed him through.
When he turns eighteen, plug the hole.
— Mark Twain

I RELATE WELL to the continuing arms reduction discussions between the superpowers. As our children grow into the adolescent years, the missiles seem to be flying through our house with increased regularity.

One that was well-targeted came from my oldest daughter one day in her twelfth year. Jamie's eyes— big and brown like her mother's—

221

had that look of warning in them that I've grown to treat with highest caution. Over the years I've often seen the same expression on her mom's face, and it always meant, "You better listen, Honey."

"Dad," Jamie said, "guess what's going to happen to you in a few months."

Mentally groping to figure out the bombshell (I hoped the IRS didn't have a problem with my latest tax return), I responded calmly, "What, Sweetheart? I don't have a clue."

Her "Beware!" look didn't change. "I'm going to turn thirteen and you're going to have a teenager on your hands."

The way she said it, I would have thought our house was about to be burglarized. I didn't know whether to panic, to board up the windows, or to borrow my brother's handcuffs and straightjacket (from his days as a policeman), and lock her up.

"A teenager, huh? Sounds like fun." It sounded crazy.

Having launched her missile— intermediate range, multiple warhead— she walked away.

THE TEENAGE YEARS. It's a time when the kids are going through so many changes— and so are their aging parents . . . a time when communicating the all-important "I believe in you" in words they understand is a challenge indeed— since Teenspeak is an altogether different language, and by the time you finally master it, it changes.

BUT THANKS to having spent much time in a laboratory with other people's teenagers— as well as having many in-depth conversations with close friends who are effectively parenting teenagers— I've discovered a few kernels of wisdom we're relying on to help us make this stage in our kids' growth a satisfying adventure for all of us.

Here's a condensed list of those principles. I offer them in the hope that they help you bring out the best during your children's teen years.

Every parent is naturally stronger in some of these areas than in others, and we tend to emphasize too much what we're good at. If we're merciful, we tend to be a pushover and let the kids run the house. If we're well-disciplined, we tend to beat our kids to death with rules and reminders. The word BALANCE needs to plated with 24-karat gold and hung over the bathroom mirror for every Mom and Dad to read each morning.

1. CALLOUSED KNEES

With a new teenager I realized all over again how the job of parenting was a lot bigger than my abilities. That means a lot of prayer.

The Lord says, "You have not because you ask not," and "Ask, and you will receive, that your joy may be full." I figure that if one prayer is good, a thousand would be great. In this critical matter of raising teenagers, I want to get as close as possible to achieving Paul's directive to "Pray without ceasing."

We can expect to have Jamie at home for

only six teenage years. So for six years, I will concentrate in prayer for her . . . asking God to make them *six golden years.*

We ask with faith. God can do it. As Romans 8:32 suggests, if God thought enough of us to give us His Son, won't He also give us all things— including the wisdom and strength and love to help her make the most of this season in her life?

So we pray. We pray for all the people in her life: her friends, her teammates, her teachers and coaches, her future husband. We pray for her ability to withstand peer pressure. We pray for her self-image. We pray for her desire to honor and obey us. We pray for our wisdom in guiding her. And I pray that the example of my life will be more consistently godly.

2. ELEPHANT EARS

The teen years demand a parent who's eager to listen, slow to speak, and full of understanding. Every teenager is different, and getting to know them well means a lot of listening and learning.

One of our daughters talks about everything (and I mean everything). The other is much quieter. We try to be prepared constantly to enter an open door into her heart whenever she's in the mood to share her thoughts and feelings. These opportunities come at the most unexpected times . . . and often involve hurt or crisis. When these moments come, I want to be ready.

3. HEART TO HEART

In these crazy years, my relationship with her is everything. When trendy music and the media are telling her the way to have fun is through sex and drugs and alcohol, and when peers are telling her parents are no longer relevant . . . I want to be the person she loves being with the most.

When I'm going to run errand, I invite her to come along. When her basketball team has a game, I want to be there. If I'm speaking at a youth rally, there's a place for her on "the team" that's putting it on. When she comes home from a party, her "late date" is with me.

A few years ago, a good buddy of mine (and an excellent counselor of teens) was leading a parenting seminar at our camp during a 24-hour Parents' Day at the end of their children's two-week camp session. He was talking about some of the principles in this book when a father's hand shot up in protest near the back of the room.

"Yes sir, do you have a question?" my friend asked.

The man stood up, clearing his throat with deliberateness. "You may talk about all this theoretical hodge-podge," he said, "but when it comes to reality, that kind of thing just doesn't fly."

Other parents who were successfully applying these principles took the challenge off my friend's hands, and told the man how they had seen them work in their own homes. The man quieted down, but at dinner after the seminar he and his wife encountered my friend again with more rebuttal.

It just so happened that later that night his son was to be competing in a camp swim meet. Also that night, the United States basketball team was playing in a televised game at the Olympics. As they were talking with my friend, the man looked at his watch and said suddenly, "Good grief, Honey, we've got to get back to the motel. Tip-off time for the game is in fifteen minutes."

Of course these principles my friend was discussing were hodge-podge in that man's home.

Olympic basketball games may come only every four years, but when you need to spend time with your kids there are always enough excuses and distractions around to keep you from it. No matter how eloquently we phrase our excused absences, adolescents especially have a built-in baloney detector. To them, our actions give a loud and clear signal: You're only priority #37 in my life.

4. PENETRATING EYES

The most important people for a teenager's parents to know are that teen's friends. The Bible declares that "bad company corrupts good morals." I've seen it happen a thousand times to need no convincing that it's as infallible as every other biblical truth. "When you lay down with dogs," the saying goes, "you get fleas."

So I want to know the *character* of my

daughter's friends— to know them down to their very marrow. My daughter goes out with good friends, or she doesn't go. It's a ground rule. If she wants to "hang out" with friends we don't know yet, then they "hang out" at our house. We talk to them and try to become their friends as well. We also make telephone calls and find out more about them.

The earlier you begin this with your kids, the more success you'll have with it.

5. MANNEQUIN BODY

Teenagers are notorious experts on their parents' weakness. That fact doesn't demand our perfection, but it does demand our giving strict attention to our habits, especially in the critical area of how we treat our bodies. For my daughter's sake, then, as well as for my wife and the other kids and myself as well, I'm cranking up the example on this one!

Be fully aware that the really "in" things for most teenagers are getting high with drugs and alcohol. If I pop pills (prescription or not), why can't they pop pills (prescription or not)? If I drink a beer to relax, why can't they have one— or even smoke a joint— to take the edge off their anxieties? If you haven't already discovered it the hard way, as have so many couples whom I've observed in the aftershock, the "legal" issue just doesn't fly with teenagers nowadays. They're too discerning — and too logical— not to see through it. A friend of mine recently confronted his fifteen-year-old daughter with the legal aspect of her drinking bouts, and she snapped back, "Why don't you drive fifty-five?"

The same logic applies in every aspect of our behavior. If we tell little lies (which may be larger than we admit), why can't they tell little lies (which may be larger than they admit). If my wife and I rent an R-rated video, why can't they watch one at a theater? If I pay to see and hear performers talk and act immorally, what's so wrong with teenagers talking the same language and acting out the same scenes with their friends?

Kids measure our values by how we spend our time and how we spend our money— not by what we preach.

6. STEADY HAND

A steady hand is one that's careful with handouts.

It's no longer in fashion to say No to your children, but we don't pay much attention to fashion in our home. The "extras" in life that my daughter legitimately desires are not hers simply for the asking. Privileges come with proven responsibility. Freedom always travels with accountability. Payment is the reward for hard work. Giving will be mutual. More giving will always follow the evidence of gratitude.

I owe my daughter a bed.

I owe her adequate food.

I owe her an educational opportunity.

I owe her a good home.

I owe her a sound example of godly living.

I owe her a biblical foundation for life.

But the accessories are privileges to be earned. Talking on the phone (which I pay for) is a privilege. Going out at night (and keeping me up) is a privilege. Spending five dollars (that I have earned) at McDonald's is a privilege.

If you feel your adolescent is beginning to kick against the restraining walls and needs to understand in more detail the freedom/ responsibility balance, you may want to use the six-level system shown on the following pages, a system that many parents have adopted in various forms. The presentation here is only a suggested guideline. I strongly recommend that you draw up your own system of levels that meet with your particular standards.

The great thing about a system such as this is that the child can choose the level on which they decide to live— having whatever freedoms they choose to have, but always with the corresponding responsibilities.

☜

FREEDOMS AND RESPONSIBILITIES — Six Levels

Level 1

Living in a youth detention home— no freedom. The psychologists and authorities decide everything.

Level 2

Living at home, but with no freedom— no phone use, no money to spend, no nights out. We take you to school, and we pick you up after school. Weekends are spent at home.

Level 3

FREEDOMS

A. One 5-minute phone call per night.
B. One night out per weekend, with 11 P.M. curfew.
C. One television show (approved by us) per day.

RESPONSIBILITIES

A. Obedience to parents
B. Respect for parents evident at all times.
C. Chores done at home consistently.
D. Complete honesty with parents and teachers.
E. No use of alcohol, drugs, or tobacco.
F. Clean language at all times.
G. Social time limited to friends with good, stable reputation.

H. Let parents know specific plans— where you are and for how long— at all times.
I. No unexcused absences in school.
J. "Good deportment" slips signed weekly by teachers.
K. Grade average :

Level 4

ADDED FREEDOMS

A. Up to thirty minutes on the phone per night.
B. Curfew on weekend night out extended till midnight.
C. One night out during the week until 11 P.M.
D. Monitored spending— set at ____ per week.
E. Driving to and from school.
F. On two afternoons per week: two hours free time after school.

ADDED RESPONSIBILITIES

A. Always ready for school on time and for bed on time, without parental reminders.
B. Extra help provided regularly for Mom and Dad in housework, yardwork, etc.
C. Daily quiet time with God
D. Regular attendance at church.
E. Regular attendance at church youth meetings.
F. Grade average :

Level 5

ADDED FREEDOMS

Increased from Level 4
in accordance with
your interests and
desires and Mom
and Dad's standards.

ADDED RESPONSIBILITIES

Increased from level
four in accordance
with your own needs
for character growth
and Mom and Dad's
standards.

Level 6

Living away from home, and able to maintain a
lifestyle reflecting high moral values.

—21—

Crossroads

Time. Time. Waiting. Waiting.

Movement. Wonder.

Waiting. Waiting.

Waiting.

Pangs. Hospital. Nurses. Pangs. Fear. Pressure.
Hurt. Breathing. Timing. Time.

Waiting. Patience. Husband. Close. Sharing.

Pain. Pain!

Increased.

Pain!

Intense. *PAIN!* Doctor!

PAIN!

Push! Pain. *Push!*

Birth!

Life . . .

A child. Ours. Healthy. Beautiful.

Tears. Beginning. Dreams. Sharing. Happy. Telephone.

Ours. Likeness. Tiny. Mystery. Eyes — Mom's. Fingers — Dad's. Mouth — Grandma's. Nose — Grandpa's.

Rest. Plans. Dreams. Nursing. Rest. Dreams. Hopes. Talking. Laughing. Sharing. Tomorrow.

Home. Us.

Crying. Feeding. Diapers. Schedule. Crying. Feeding. Diapers. Night. Tired. Late. Early. Rash. Reality.

Tiny. Warm. Cuddling. Ours! Dreams. Future.

Days. Weeks. Months.

Everyday. New. Recognition. Smiles. Sounds. Playful. Sitting. Crawling. Giggling. Close. Hugs. Tomorrow.

Step. Fall. Step. Steps. Good! Yes! Steps. Stumble. Steps. *Yes!* Success. Dreams. Plans.

Year. Years.

Talk. Play. Run. Sing. Make. Climb. Laugh. Grow.

Questions. Questions. Questions. God. Where?
Heaven. Heart. Ask. Jesus. Loves. Me.

Begin. School. Teacher. Bus. New. Playground.
Friends. Fun. Acceptance. Rejection. Hurt.
Questions.

Home. Hugs. Talk. Bedside. Pray. Snug. Sleep.

While. You. Quietly. Watching.
Praying.
Dreams.

Morning.
Love. Encourage. Discipline. Hug. Love.
Live. Example. Pray.
Meals. Hands. Held. Hearts. Warm.
Scripture. Pray. Play. Work. Together.
Talk. Listen.
Show. Share. Shape.

Summers. Winters. Years.

TV. Funny. Flashy. Smart.
"Love." Sex. Drinks. Smiles. Laughs. Lies.
Tough. Faces. Hate. Blood. Crash. Kill.
Buy. Buy. Buy. Buy. Happy. Happy.
Lies.
NO!

Taller. Stronger. Learning. Helping. Wondering.
Wrong. Right. Growing. Going. Strong.

You. Work. Climb. Push. Go.
House. Committees. Clubs. Go. Status. Climb. Mine.
Go. Go.

> Stretched. Thin. Tight. Fatigue.
> Questions. No. Together. No.
> Spend. Time. With. No.

Not. Fair.
Why?

Why?

Get. Attention.

> No!
> Lose. Temper.
> Harsh. Hurt.
> NO!

> No . . .
> Stop. Wrong.
> Forgive. Me.
> Let's . . .

> *Back. Up. Back. Together.*
> *Back. Yard. Talk.*
> *Listen. Listen. Laugh. Hug.*
> *Change.*
> *Mend.*
> *I. Really. Love. You.*

Vacation? Really? Away. Together. Us.
Great. Time. See. Do. Explore. Great.
Back. Home. Different. Great!
Back. To school.

Taller. Stronger. Different. Body. Changing.
Questions. Parties. Peers. First. Date. Weekends.

Wild. Challenge. Just. Try. Everybody. Does.
Music. Movies. Cars. More. After. Impress. Just. Watch.
Wild. Go. Get. Be. Free. Cool. Why. Not?

Fun. Fun? Free. Free?
Me. Who? How? When? Where? Am. I. Need.
What? Who? She. He. They. Me. Who? Where?
Am. I. Need. What? Who? Need. Time. Time.

Out. Late. Come. Home. Still. Up? Time. Milk.
Cookies. Talk . . .

Listen. Listen. Love. Encourage. Listen.
Think. Listen.
Offer. Ideas. Listen. Goals. Listen. Plans. Listen.
I. Love. You. Are. So. Special.
Listen. Listen. Time. Time.
Good. Night. Lights. Out. Quietly.
Praying.
Praying.

Time. Time. Time. Together. Plans. Together.
Work. Together. Dreams. Together. Getting . . .

Ready.

Graduation!

Leaving. Home.

Ready.

Ready.

Gone.

A child.
Ours. Healthy. Beautiful.
Remember? Birth! Life . . . A child. Ours. Likeness.
Sharing. Dreams. Future.
Time. Time. Time.

Time.

Ready?

Gone.

⚷

PART V

Tomorrow's Family Album

"I'm glad you're home!"

—22—

The Generation That Followed Discovery

WE HAVE IT ALL!

We have within us a God-given desire for intimacy with our children, plus an innate yearning to carve our initials on their hearts as a lasting legacy— lending our dreams and values for building the trustworthy foundation of future generations.

Most of us have a satisfactory paycheck in return for a workweek that usually is significantly shorter than that of our forefathers. We have both time and money to enjoy recreation together as a family, and an occasional vacation.

We have the Bible and the Holy Spirit of God for daily guidance.

And we have our country's most valuable resource— not oil or gold or wheat . . . but the home. The home— built around the marriage relationship that God gave us as a glimpse into the mysterious union between Christ Himself and the church. Home— the most powerful place in the world.

To help us make that place the best it can possibly be, the resources available through youth ministries and parents' support groups are more abundant now than in all the previous generations combined.

We have unparalleled possibilities for fulfillment. Our treasure is vast . . . but not necessarily permanent. We can waste and lose it— like the people of Greece and Rome— or, as the people of God we were meant to be, we can channel these true riches into the lives of our children.

If we truly make the Discovery of how valuable these kids are, and how vast their potential that we release by loving them totally . . . then the generation that follows Discovery will be like no other this world has seen.

Our sons and daughters can have the privilege, more than any other generation in history, of living life with all the joy and discipline and love and satisfaction that we were created to enjoy. They can be like a forest of unprecedented majesty, full of lush, towering trees that teem with fruitful branches.

Is THIS JUST fruit pie in the sky?

I don't think so. Already I see so many fruit-bearing trees nearing maturity. Our neighborhood is full of them. These kids bind together like a street gang, setting the pace for Christlike living in their school and among their friends. They love being on the growing edge.

As I travel I see healthy trees rising up everywhere. Last weekend I met a high school junior who told me, "Joe, my goal is to make my school the first Christian public school in America." I didn't catch what he meant till he continued, "By the time I graduate, I want everyone in my school to know the Truth." What vision! And you can bet that boy has a mom or dad or both who stand behind him all the way.

The week before, at a youth rally in a different state, I met a high school senior whose influence resulted in thirteen new student-led Bible study groups— one on each high school campus in her city. I also know the supportive mom who launched that girl's dream.

In the same city, a student body president sent birthday cards— loaded with scriptural truth— to all 1,500 kids in his high school.

I talk with hundreds of kids every year who say to their parents "Please" and "Thank you" and "Yes sir" and "Yes ma'am, I'll be happy to"— not

out of fear, but out of a healthy respect for
authority.

These kids may not be a great majority. But
there is a growing "Who's Who in Moral Values,"
kids who lock elbows and encourage each other to
say No to drugs, alcohol, and sex.

And there can be more.

I've seen a runaway sixteen-year-old come
home to his daddy's smile and open arms.

I've marveled as a strung-out father
revamped his lifestyle and work schedule to spend
more time at home during his children's growing-
up years.

I've seen parent and child embrace after
they've really discovered each other at a camp or
during a church retreat or on the other side of a
tragedy.

And I've felt a quickened heartbeat after
seeing one of my own children suppress natural,
self-centered desires and instead imitate Christ in
a critical area of life.

I hope that you, too, have a glimpse of the
unfathomable riches of these things that give life
such a passion.

The resources, the riches, the momentum
. . . we've got to believe it will work, and harness
all that energy.

The search for something better can help make it happen— the sheer frustration of trying to find happiness and fulfillment through chemicals or sex outside marriage or fame or fortune; the nagging fear about AIDS; the rising disillusionment with the New Age; the utter emptiness of passing fads.

Sure, outside pressures counterattack with relentless force.

But I believe that by far the great majority of children who are given at least one good adult friend who has made the Discovery will choose to have their own personal walk with Jesus Christ, and to pattern their life after His.

And the generation that follows Discovery will be a pleasure indeed to live in.

☞

—23—

Dancing

The older I get, the luckier I am.
— Bill Cosby

I KNOW IT HAS ONLY BEEN through God's amazing grace that I can ever call myself a parent— especially one whose crown is adorned with four children I've been admiring almost heroically the more I get to know them.

Tonight as I tucked my oldest in bed (I guess they'll never ougrow that as long as they live in this house) we spent our usual fifteen to twenty minutes together— praying, memorizing and reviewing Scripture, and discussing the day's events. Tonight was unusually special. Jamie began to ask questions about her professional career that looms in the not-so-distant future (I still can't believe the years have passed by so quickly). Later, something she prayed moved me to gratitude. "Dear Jesus," she said, "thank you for Mom and Dad who love me so much. I want to be just like them someday."

247

I reflected for a few moments on our thousands of bedtime talks and the hunk of Scripture we've committed to memory. I thought back on all our daddy-kid days . . . the countless gymnastics meets and volleyball games . . . the family trips far and wide . . . and the tearful hugs that followed some significant spankings. I thought of the "imbalance" of my life— weighted toward time with my kids and away from any hobbies and interests outside the home. I smiled . . . knowing I wouldn't trade any of these times for any presidential office or a six-figure paycheck.

I looked at my little prize snuggled in her feather pillow, and said to her, "Peanut, thanks for saying that. But there's something you need to know. I've always looked up to you. You're one hundred times better than I ever dreamed of being. You'll do things in your lifetime I couldn't begin to do.

"And I've loved every minute of being your daddy."

THERE'S A LOT ABOUT HEAVEN I don't know yet, but I do know enough to be sure I want to spend eternity there.

I'm also certain— and for this, Dear God, I'll be forever grateful— that four kids and their mom

cel•e•brate \sĕl-ĭ-brāt\ *v.* 1. To jump for joy and leap with laughter. 2. To hang balloons and make ballyhoo; to have fun and play games. 3. To kiss and make up.

and one lucky dad are going to be there singing and dancing through those golden streets, laughing over the great family memories we've known in this house.

If you feel in your heart a new flicker of light and warmth for those you love most . . . then by all means fan the flame. Pour your creative energies into building up the blaze, and let it rage. Put your entire heart into your home, and watch the family scrapbook thicken with happy pages.

If you have a prodigal son or daughter, I pray you will know soon the euphoric rush of unimagined magnificence as that child returns to renew the closeness you once shared.

And if you have a spouse at home, I hope you'll make the soap operas blush as you pour yourself into that relationship.

Parenting wasn't designed as an experience to simply survive. We were meant to *celebrate* it . . . to succeed in it . . . to weep in both the hurts and the joys . . . and leave nothing behind to regret.

⚷

—24—

Discovery at Dawn

*A life is made up of a great number of small incidents
and a small number of great ones.*
— Roald Dahl

Blessed are the pure in heart, for they shall see God.
— Matthew 5:8

I'VE SEEN A BRIDE— or was it an angel?—
adorned in pure white, radiant as she made her
once-in-a-lifetime journey down the aisle. When
her slender hands took mine and she pledged her
lifelong troth to me, I felt the way the first man to
land on the moon must have felt. How beautiful
was that day . . . and how undeserving was I of
such a prize!

And when that little bride gave birth to my
first baby girl, I saw the miracle of life. Air filled
her lungs. Light invaded her squinting eyes. And

251

rushing through the countless miles of capillaries in her precious, tiny body was blood carrying the mingled genetic codes of hundreds of generations of bride and groom.

I've seen God intertwining my heart with my daughter's in a response as continuing as the ocean tides . . . then doing it once again with another precious child, and another, and another.

I've been fortunate to witness tears of intense relief and happiness as teenage drug addicts and young prostitutes and prisoners find hope and life, all in a moment of renewal from God. It is indeed a miraculous sight to see a tiny seed slowly rupture and give way to rootlet and stem, and later become a sapling, and in time a timber giant to cradle children in its branches; but to see a dead tree come back to life is so much the greater miracle.

I've watched the veil between time and eternity lift with wondrous ease as a fulfilled but fatigued old granddad tenderly closed his eyelids one last time, in a moment of timeless peace.

---

home \hōm\ *n.* 1. A special place of refuge that harbors me *in,* and shuts *out* hurtful forces from the outside world. 2. Where pleasures meet you at the door—the smell of cookies baking . . . Mom's hug and Dad's smile . . . "I'm so glad you're home!" 3. Where no one yells at me. 4. Where hearts dwell truly in love. 5. What forever's for.

TODAY AT DAWN came another discovery, as
ten thousand shades of color were programmed
into my eyes. In the minutes before sunrise, with
a whisper of cirrus clouds lacing the eastern sky
and cotton puffs of cumulus dancing nearby,
morning's first rays sprayed their edges with a
garden variety of reds and golds. Then, in a
twinkling of an eye, a brilliant goldmine erupted.
The fiery suncrest peeked over the mountain,
inflaming the autumn hues of Ozark mountain
foliage: from the orange and yellow of sassafras to
the deep burgundy of black gum, with Indian-red
sumac and multi-shaded maples and a hundred
others.

I watched in amazement. Just for me, the
Creator had painted a work of art unmatched in
all the galleries of the world. I remembered the
words of an old Galilean fisherman: "We were
eyewitnesses of His majesty."

With that dazzling display lighting the way,
my mind raced straight and sure to my most
prized possessions: my bride, having become even
more beautiful in the twenty fleeting years I've
known her . . . the growing foursome who crown
my life with significance by calling me Daddy . . .
my aging mom and dad who never grow weary of
being my number one fans.

It was more than just another indescribable
Ozark October sunrise. It was a rediscovery of the
designer label that has trademarked my life since
the time when there was no time . . . not the
label of some Paris textile guru, but of the Great
Designer of a universe infinite and infinitesimal,
where millions of galaxies are born at the blinking

of His eye, and where the minds of Plato and Socrates are baffled by the metamorphosis of a helpless, ugly caterpillar into a butterfly dressed more beautifully than any queen who ever reigned.

I was personally designed, planned, and programmed to know this Creator . . . to know Him with greater intimacy and completeness than I know my wife (who to this day puts butterflies into flight formation in my stomach whenever she holds my hand). I was designed for fulfillment— not any cheap, add-water-and-stir euphoria over a new title or promotion, a bigger paycheck, a sensual encounter, or an acquired jewel, but true, lasting fulfillment.

I, like you, am designed by God for the Eternal . . .

And His plan was for me

to receive it from a mom and dad,

to participate in it with my bride,

and (the most exciting adventure of all!)

to pass it on to my children.

JUST AS THE DAWN'S DESIGNER gave me renewed perspective on my family life with this morning's sunrise . . . so I now pass this fulfilling focus on to you. It is appropriately mixed with tears and hugs and laughter and the holding of little hands around the dinner table, thanking Him for the experience.

I hope to rekindle the embers that give your life its greatest purpose. As you long to fulfill your part in the design, and to face successfully the countless challenges that come in every family, I pray that what you have read on these pages will stay always with you, offering answers . . . solutions . . . and hope.

⚷